D1040243

Together Resilient

Together Resilient:
Building Community in the
Age of Climate Disruption

Ma'ikwe Ludwig

for Jibran, Andrew, Nandi,
Abby, Noah, and Nebiyat

for your sakes,
I hope I am wrong about the worst of it
and right about the best of it

—ML

Contents

Foreword

I am happy to be supporting this book with its vitally needed message. Ma'ikwe and I share a commitment to building cooperative culture. For the past 40 years, I and my organisation Local Futures have raised awareness about the fundamental importance of community, about the importance of rebuilding close webs of social support.

I came to this conclusion because of experiences in Ladakh or "Little Tibet." In 1975 I was asked to accompany a film team to this remote region in the Himalayas. In my work as a linguist I had travelled to many parts of the world, but nothing had prepared me for what I encountered in Ladakh. High up on the Tibetan plateau, I came to know a people who had never been colonised or "developed," and were still living according to their own values and principles. Despite a harsh and barren environment, people were prospering both materially and, more significantly, emotionally.

Before coming to Ladakh I had studied psychology at university, where I'd been led to believe that certain features of human nature—greed, fear, and competitiveness in particular—lay behind most of society's ills. Yet after being in Ladakh, I began to see that Western culture *distorts* human nature. It breeds separation, competition, and a self-conscious need to keep proving ourselves.

As it became clearer to me that it is our global, industialized consumer culture that makes us feel out of place and disconnected, I felt a sense of relief. It was deeply healing to discover that so much of our psychological unrest (including my own sense of displacement) came from a culture out of balance, rather than an intrinsic human flaw.

In Ladakh, well-being was maintained through intimate daily contact between people and the natural world; and through knowledge about one's immediate environment with its changing seasons, needs, and limitations. The "environment" was not some alien, problematic sphere of human concern; it was where people lived. The understanding that was gained through a life rooted in the natural world created a sense of kinship with plants and animals. I saw how the profound psychological security that was gained through community and a deep contact with nature fostered tolerance and openness toward others.

The traditional spiritual teachings were a reminder of belonging: a reminder of our inextricable interdependence one with another and with everything in the cosmos. This message was ever present in community life, in a way of living in which you knew that you could depend on others to lend a helping hand. In rituals and in words of wisdom, passed on from the elders to the young ones, the importance of interdependence was constantly reinforced.

Spending time with Ladakhi families, I saw how children were brought up in an enveloping network of extended family, friends, plants, and animals. My close friend Dolma, for example, spent much time with her baby boy Angchuk, but caring for the baby was not her job alone, everyone looked after babies. Even the teenage boys from next door were not embarrassed to be seen cooing over little Angchuk or rocking him to sleep with a lullaby. This brought out the boys' ability to care and nurture—qualities that were embraced, rather than rejected, by masculine identities.

Children were not segregated into peer groups; they grew up surrounded by people of all ages, from young babies to great-grandparents. Education was the product of an intimate relationship with the community and its environment. Children learned from grandparents, family, and friends about connections, process, and change, and about the intricate web of fluctuating relationships in the natural world around them. When villagers gathered to discuss important issues or had festivals and parties, children of all ages were present, observing the processes or partaking in the festivities until they simply dropped off to sleep.

Old people also participated in all spheres of life. For the elderly in Ladakh there were no years of staring into space, unwanted and alone; old age implied years of valuable experience and wisdom. There was no hurry to life, so if grandparents worked more slowly it did not matter. One of the main reasons old people remained so alive and involved was their constant contact with the young. The very oldest and the very youngest formed a special bond; they were often best friends.

Life in traditional Ladakh stands in stark contrast with the typical Western experience of growing up and ageing. Within almost every family, the economic pressures on parents systematically rob them of time with their children. As a consequence, more and more young children are relegated to the care of strangers in crowded day-care centres. Older children are often left in the company of violent video games or the corporate sponsors of their favourite television shows. Flesh-and-blood role models—parents and grandparents, aunts and uncles, friends and neighbours—that children once looked up to, are replaced with media and advertising images: glamorous movie and rock stars, steroid-enhanced athletes, and airbrushed supermodels. Time spent in nature—fundamentally important to our psychological wellbeing—is increasingly rare.

The globalised consumer culture disconnects us from one another and from the natural world, blinding us to what is essential for happiness and wellbeing. It destabilises our sense of belonging—to community, to place, to the earth—and replaces stable senses of self with insecure identities created through consumer products and images.

All around the world, people are beginning to understand that, in order to wean ourselves from our personally, as well as ecologically, destructive consumer addictions, we need to rebuild structures that support a sense of belonging, and allow us to see our impact on others and on the natural world.

Intentional communities play a central role in this process—as beacons of hope to societies that have lost their way. They are part of a larger, world-wide movement towards "localisation"—reweaving the fabric of place-based culture. These movements are rooted in people's desire to preserve the bonds to family, community, and nature that make life meaningful. They are the foundation for a new—and ancient—future.

Across the globe, people are demonstrating incredible wisdom, courage, and perseverance and have shown me that feelings of fear, isolation, and discontent are actually a natural reaction to a system gone awry. From these feelings springs the search for what is real, healthy, and essential for life. They give us the inspiration to work together with those who have already started the journey to reclaim health, security, and joy.

This book offers an important roadmap to help us regain our humanity—to find our home in the living world around us.

Helena Norberg-Hodge
March, 2017

Acknowledgments

On Dec. 5, 2014, Christopher Kindig, the Business Manager of the Fellowship for Intentional Community, sent me a blandly titled email: "book idea." In it, he proposed that I write a book about community that the FIC would publish and sell. The project got delayed by a year, mostly because I was crazy busy doing a national speaking tour that year about Dancing Rabbit Ecovillage, community living, and climate change, and developing the main themes of this book along the way. But eventually, that first email led to the book you are holding in your hands. So first and foremost, I thank Christopher for his faith in me and urging me to produce this thing. He was a help every step of the way, and deserves significant credit for this coming into being.

The rest of the FIC played along too—thanks to the Board for approving the project, Sky Blue for a hundred layers of mutual support, and my talented and blessedly easy to work with editor (for both this and my articles that pop up in *Communities* magazine), Chris Roth. Marty Klaif also deserves thanks for diligently doing the final-stage detail stuff that I have neither patience nor talent for, copy editing and typesetting this book.

Multiple people at the two main communities profiled here were of help, especially Tereza Brown and Nathan Brown at Dancing Rabbit Ecovillage, and Valerie Renwick and Misty Vredenburg at Twin Oaks Community. Brooke Jones, the Research Director at Dancing Rabbit's Center for Sustainable and Cooperative Culture, has been a friend and companion on the journey of data collection in communities, and her mentorship and numbers in that area are key elements of this book. And way back, Dr. Joshua Lockyer took an interest in DR as a place worth studying, and neither the speaking tour nor this book would have come about without his patient nurturing of that for years.

Thank you to all past and current members and residents of Dancing Rabbit Ecovillage, Twin Oaks Community, and Bhutan. This is your story in some significant ways, and I'm honored and grateful to have been able to record and share all the amazing things you are doing right.

Also formative in this book: my many years of learning and mentorship from Laird Schaub. You'd be hard pressed to cleanly separate Laird's influence out of any chapter in this book, and I'm grateful for the support to both learn, and to build on and depart from that learning—real mentors give you that space to grow in new directions, and Laird provided me that with both grace and cheerleading, if occasional eye-rolling. More recently, I'm grateful to Trish, Joe, Frankie, and Baigz of Sandhill Farm's Consent Collective for starting an anti-racism group that was extremely well-timed in my own journey. I hope you hear the echoes of your gentle pushing and clear-headed prodding in this work.

Chong Kee Tan, Bruno Seraphin, Brandy Gallagher, and Pascale Aline Bertoli all provided invaluable interviews for the book. If I got anything wrong, that's on me—these folks were fabulous. Ian McDonald provided the data on life satisfaction in community that is a key element to my constant public messaging that community living doesn't suck. And Jacob Corvidae and Tawana Petty helped me sort through the amazingness that is Detroit's food activism scene.

Bill McKibben, Naomi Klein, Dr. Viola Cordova, Ken Wilber, and Joanna Macy all deserve acknowledgment for being the main writers I've turned to the past five years for deepening understanding.

Like many a modern project, the initial production of this book was only possible through a crowdfunding campaign. Thank you so much to our donors:

Amos Alan Lans	Chris Altenbach	Jamie Gaines
Ali Kilpatrick	Chris Roth	Janel Healy
Ann Andrex	Christopher Kindig	Jackie Augustine
Andrea Patrick	Chong Kee Tan	Jacqueline Ziegler
Andy Brett Yoken	Cynthia Greene	Jayde Gaines
Aurora DeMarco	Cynthia Tina	Jean Berman
Becky Laskody	Dana Driscoll	Jenny Upton
Ben Grondahl	Daniel Greenberg	Jillian Downey
Benjamin Nelson	Deborah Altus	Joel Whiting
Betsy Morris	Deborah Gaj	John Duvall
Boris Sondagh	Diana Kirk	Jon Andelson
Bryden	Diana Sette	Jonathan Betz-Zall
Carmen Gilmore	Dick Manley	Joseph Clark
Carol Koziol	Dorothy Mazeau	Joshua Jones
Caroline Cohen	Eden Winter	Joyce Bressler
Caroline Onischak	Elizabeth Davis	Karen Parsons
Cassandra Ferrera	Ellen Kaspi	Kassia Arbabi
Cassidy Anton	Elyse Awazu	Kay Howard
Catherine Bock	Eric Chrisp	Kelly Bachman
Catherine F Stentzel	Gary Bachman	Kerri Smith

Laura Miller
Laurie Simons
Loren Schein
Malcolm Sanforde
Maria Jensen
Marjorie Alexander
Martin Adams
Marty Klaif
Mary Ann Clark
Mary Pierce
Meade Sparks
Melissa Oliver
Molly Hatfield
Nancy Simmers

Nick Joyce
Peter Gringinger
Raines Cohen
Ray Teurfs
Richard Grossman
Robert Hoffman
Robert Lyons
Roger Stube
Roy Greene
Sara Rose
Seth Wilpan
Shannon Farm
Community
Stacy Cadence
Hilgenberg

Stephen Young
Stephanie Naftal
Susan Frank
Susan Fuhr
Tamara Hunt
Tawana Petty
Thomas Llewellyn
Tom Greene
Wendy Brawer
Wendy Pressoir
Vicki Robin
Yehudit Lieberman
Yoomie Ahn
Zach Rubin

Finally, Matt Stannard deserves far more praise than I could possibly heap at his feet. His work on economic justice and fierce insistence on finding a way to mesh ecological values and communalism has been a tremendous boon to my own development as a justice advocate. Plus, he shares his life with me, brought me chocolate and breakfast at key moments of wanting to pull my hair out with this book, and is nearly enough to make a woman believe in soul mates, were she so inclined.

Ma'ikwe Ludwig
Laramie, WY
April 2, 2017

Introduction:
The View from Cornfields

Middle America.

That phrase probably doesn't evoke images of sustainable living, and the truth is, when I looked out my windows for the eight years I lived at Dancing Rabbit Ecovillage, what I saw to the east was a typical midwestern farmer's field, complete with cows. But to the west is a carefully crafted strawbale home and vibrant organic garden, to the south, solar panels and windmills, and to the north, a swimming pond—one of the more fun ways that Rabbits share resources in the community. Despite the images it brings to mind right away, this tiny patch of middle America is a sustainable living project that may well hold the keys to our fixing the climate crisis before we take it past the point where all is lost.

Dancing Rabbit (a name called variously whimsical, ridiculous, playful, and—for some of our indigenous friends who associate the name with the ill-begotten Treaty of Dancing Rabbit Creek—racist) is a sustainable living demonstration project, located in the politically and socially conservative northeastern corner of Missouri. It may well be the premier ecovillage project in the US, an intentional community that has achieved some incredible ecological gains without disconnecting from modern life.

Bizarre though this may sound, rural Missouri is home to one of the most potent experiments in America addressing climate disruption. Climate disruption (so much more accurate of a term than the neutral sounding "climate change" or the potentially nice sounding "global warming") is the single most serious issue we are facing in the world today. The other serious challenges that confront us—and there are many, from wealth inequities to racism and sexism, to a host of other environmental issues—all fall into the category of "Stuff we won't get a chance to keep arguing about" if we don't manage to get this one right. No other issue I am aware of has a literal biological clock ticking.

So a bunch of people have gathered in the middle of what most politely call "nowhere" and their lives are an answer to the question, "What does a sustainable life actually look like in the modern world?"

My best estimate, after studying a lot of climate-related data and having conversations with others who are even more up to their eyeballs in data than I am, is this: we need to reduce carbon emissions by a whopping 90% of the current American average. And the timeline on which we need to do that has been gradually getting shorter, not just because time is progressing, but because the news seems to get worse every month as we learn more. Time is just one of the many resources we are running out of. Thus, the goal we all will need to embrace is one that Dancing Rabbit is modeling, albeit imperfectly, in present time: the magic 10% mark. And Rabbits do this while living high quality, socially connected lives—not lives of deprivation, a point I find important to make in the process of attempting to "sell" community living to Americans.

And make no mistake: my audience here *is* Americans. We have created a relatively comfortable bubble for ourselves—one which is merrily pumping out far more than our share of problem pollutants every year, including carbon emissions. I speak to Americans because we live in and benefit from (even if we don't want to) the belly of the climate beast. Changing how Americans do their lives is very much my goal with this book.

This book is about the two-fold hope that intentional communities[1] like Dancing Rabbit offer us at this time: both real climate solutions, and a more sustainable and humane refuge as things start to get bad. It is about the sobering realities that make Dancing Rabbits necessary, and the practical ways we can implement what we are learning in these communities in a variety of contexts. It is, finally, about the strange possibility that a post-apocalyptic life may just be a better life in some substantial ways for many people than the social isolation that many face trying to do life alone currently.

Throughout the book, I'll be using my former home of Dancing Rabbit Ecovillage as a primary example, even while I draw in other communities as well. Dancing Rabbit is one of the most mature and relevant ecological experiments in the US, and is a vivid illustration of the power and promise of intentional communities as a model for a new world.

And that promise runs deep, if we are willing to step up to the challenges of our time. I believe the intentional communities movement needs to progress beyond being a series of loosely connected, locally-specific projects and into something that truly is a movement: a sea-change in how

---

[1] Intentional communities are groups of people who choose to live together based on shared values. There are many types of intentional communities: ecovillages, communes, cohousing, cooperatives, house-shares, monasteries, and ashrams (plus plenty of groups that defy or resist labeling and simply live together) all make up what is generally considered the intentional communities movement. Depending on how broadly you define things, it may also include Amish and Mennonite communities, retirement homes, college dorms, ship's crews, summer camps, the military, and a bunch of other manifestations of people sharing resources, services, labor, philosophies, experiences, or simply a roof over their heads: certainly all of these have some things strongly in common with what is more commonly accepted as an intentional community.

we live and interrelate. Community has the potential to move us from an unsustainable culture to a sustainable one, and from an ever-more precarious economic system to a deeply stable and nurturing way of being that meets our needs far more humanely.

This is about surviving climate disruption, but it is also about more than that: the world I envision is a spiritually satisfying world of true ecological, economic, and social justice and balance. Community is one essential building block of that world, and it is that piece of the puzzle that this book is about.

Chapter 1 defines the territory of the book: a little about climate disruption and the American status quo, and more about the frameworks that I'm using to build the case for community. I'll go through the Global Ecovillage Network's framework for understanding the multiple dimensions of sustainability, look at Joanna Macy's important work on successful social movements, and then close with a look at why communities can do some interesting things in the arena of reinventing our lives that individuals or more mainstream social change groups can't.

Chapter 2 focuses on the ways that communities are already providing models of low-carbon living. In addition to Dancing Rabbit and other traditional intentional communities, we will look at modern American eco-nomads, a transformed village in the UK, and a techno-Millennialist project-in-the-making and what these different models have to bring to the table.

Chapter 3 is about all the ways that community is a potent and important tool for surviving the breakdown of both human systems (economics, for instance) and ecological systems. We'll look at the question of why more communal is better in a host of ways, and I make the case for income sharing in community as a particularly potent tool for reducing your carbon footprint quickly. We also look at resilience and security, and what they mean in the age of climate disruption.

Chapter 4 is about starting a residential intentional community with a good chance of success. It looks at the challenges and development models for new communities, and offers perspective from many years of starting and observing communities. We also explore why regionally connected networks may be better than each community being fully self-sufficient.

The rest of the book broadens the conversation back out to the wider cultural and political context. Chapter 5 focuses on the American competitive, individualistic culture and the ways we need to foster a healthy cooperative culture in order to get the world we want. It also looks closely at one particular aspect of that cultural training: the denial and devaluing of emotional work. Finally, I emphasize the ways that emotional work, particularly as it relates to climate disruption, and to race and class dynamics, is an essential building block for this new culture.

Chapter 6 looks at the broader legal and economic context that communities find themselves in, and offers a concrete reform platform for a world more conducive to citizen-led, grassroots solutions (including, but certainly not limited to, intentional communities) to the worst problems of our day.

Chapter 7 introduces our final case study, the country of Bhutan, and considers whether a whole country could qualify as an intentional community. It also looks at emotional well-being in community. Finally, the afterword is a brief call to action for my fellow community folks.

In multiple places in the book, I address community-building outside of residential groups. One of the real drawbacks to starting anew is that a tremendous amount of resources is already invested in infrastructure in the US; creating *community where you are* (to use a phrase the Fellowship for Intentional Community[2] uses) can be a powerful and financially accessible way for community to be deepened and carbon footprints lowered. Thus, I am doing my best here to model a non-dogmatic, flexible approach to applying what we've learned in residential intentional communities over the years.

---

[2] www.ic.org. FIC is an umbrella organization that works with all types of intentional communities, primarily in North America, from ecovillages to cohousing, student co-ops to communes. FIC's resources include *Communities* magazine, the Communities Directory, and their online Bookstore, selling a variety of titles of interest to people living in, and intrigued with, cooperative living.

Chapter 1: Defining the Territory

The challenges presented to us by the triple crises of climate disruption, resource scarcity, and economic insecurity have different solutions for different populations in the world. Our goal should be a sustainable[3] and low-carbon, socially equitable, high quality of life for everyone in the world. For the poorest countries, where basic human needs are yet to be met for many people, a rise in quality of life may take more resources than are currently flowing to (or staying in, as the case may be) these countries. For the wealthiest nations, we need a significant reduction in our consumption, with a parallel redefinition of what "quality of life" means.

This graph[4] does a good job of summarizing the two directions we need to be heading to meet in the middle:

Living Laboratories for a Sustainable Future

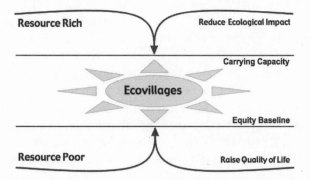

---

[3] The word "sustainable" has gotten a bit of a bad rap recently. The basic objection is that some people seem to use the word to mean "to sustain our current heavily consumptive lifestyle without having to question it" (e.g., using solar panels to simply replace coal-fired electricity generation, without also reducing how much electricity is needed). It has become code in some places for "let's sustain the status quo." That is definitely not what I mean when I use the word. What I mean is "able to be sustained into the foreseeable future without compromising future generations' ability to do the same." That is definitely not business as usual for America. It is much closer to the indigenous perspective of considering the next seven generations in everything we do.

[4] Thanks to Daniel Greenberg, a fellow ecovillage enthusiast and educator, and Earth Deeds for this graphic.

The simplest (and mostly accurate) way to read this is that the "developed" world needs to bring our overall ecological footprint down to be within the carrying capacity of the planet, in order to make space for the "developing" world to be able to bring their standard of living up to something much closer to an equitable distribution of resources. It will not be possible for everyone to live as Americans and Europeans currently do, nor is it necessary for the poorest of the poor to see no improvement in their circumstances. And ecovillages (including large-scale eco-cities) are one powerful and tested way to have these ends meet.

Here's an interesting thing, though, that this graph doesn't capture: as poor people tend to understand much better than wealthy people, community is part of what gets us through when resources are scarce.

Quality of life is partly about social connectivity, and this is never reflected in statistics like gross domestic product. In fact, GDP tends to do better in times when community is suffering. In some cases, the true quality-of-life discrepancies between rich and poor are made to look worse by the statistics because we are measuring the wrong things—in other words, a lot of rich people might not be having as good a time of it as the statistics indicate, and a lot of poor people might actually have pretty good lives in non-material ways: Is the quality of life of a socially isolated, depressed wealthy person really that much higher—or higher at all—than that of someone scraping by financially with a lot of social connection?

Of course the ideal is that we all have enough of both: ease in getting our material needs met *and* social connection. We have very few models for what that looks like. Instead, we have parodies of ease in places like the US, and lives reduced to statistics in places like Africa and India that are losing community quickly while being pushed into modernization (the end game of which is supposed to look something like what we have in the US).

The need to reverse these trends has become more urgent because climate disruption has kicked in in earnest. The Paris Climate Talks in 2016 ended with an agreed-upon goal of trying to limit overall rise in temperature to 2 degrees Celsius (about 3.6 degrees Fahrenheit) above pre-industrial levels. That sounds small, but we are already about halfway there in terms of the change in overall global average temperatures (somewhere around 1 degree C rise so far) and we are seeing unprecedented floods, drought, and wildfires, and severe weather of all sorts. Getting twice as bad as what we are seeing now would be very bad indeed.

Unfortunately, most people paying attention to what's happened since the talks are pretty sure we are going to blow past the 2 degree mark. Left unchecked, the sum of our current lifestyles on the planet yields predictions from scientists in the range of 6 to 11 degrees C in temperature rise. And our lifestyles are at the root of it: all use of fossil fuels feeds in some way or another, directly or indirectly, into someone's lifestyle. That's why there is so much focus on *per capita* emissions: because at the end of all the burning of fuels, there are people getting something out of it.

We hear about China a lot, and many nations in the developed world are taken to task (appropriately so) for their excessive contributions to the problem of climate change. And yet the most dramatic shifts in carbon emissions are happening in neither places: Mozambique, for instance, saw the biggest rise in emission between 1996 and 2006, a stunning 365% per capita...and they are still at only .24 tons per person. That's an example of a country trying to bring up their standard of living, and seeing a parallel rise in emissions.

In fact, one of the best predictors of carbon emission is income level, and you'll notice in this chart that Mozambique's number is actually below the low income point on the chart:

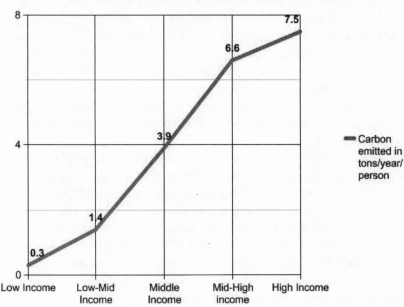

Carbon Emissions Per Capita, Worldwide by Income Level, 2013

Data: World Bank Group, Graph: Ma'ikwe Ludwig

The takeaway from that graph is this: poor people are generally not the problem.

This means that the wealthier among us (both individually and as societies) have more work to do in cleaning up our acts. That said, there are tremendous wealth inequalities within the US, and poor Americans contribute a lot less to these problems than well-off Americans do. Still, I am going to maintain that the fundamentals of the American lifestyle, in which all of us in the US participate to some degree or another, are a core problem.

I also believe strongly that poorer people have a lot more to gain (and a lot less to lose) by considering intentional community as a viable and sensible lifestyle choice. If you are poor, you might not look at community as a way of reducing your ecological footprint so much as a way to increase your economic security. Thus, while there is absolutely nuance in the term "Americans" I'm going to stick with it as a blanket term for the people I am mostly speaking to and about in this book, and assume you will relate to it as is appropriate and useful for your current circumstances.

Understanding the Problem(s)

The first major article I remember reading about climate change was a cover story from *Time* magazine in 1987. I was 17 years old, and was coming of age at the same time that the issue was just hitting the public sphere in a major way.[5] That year was one blip in what I refer to as "the incredible shrinking timeline."

You see, we've had climate scientists since the 1800s. And in the 1800s, when the Industrial Revolution was really just getting cranking, the possibility that greenhouse gases might change something significant in our world was mostly a speculative curiosity—some very cutting edge scientists said it then, but not enough research was being done for that concept to get much traction. By 1970, the year I was born, it was already clear that the greenhouse effect (as it was then dubbed) was going to have some serious negative consequences, and yet those consequences were still talked about as if they were many generations down the road.

By the early 2000s, we had started to see the front edge of serious effects, but mostly in developing nations with very little political influence internationally, and—in my mind, not coincidentally—populated largely by brown people. To anyone seriously paying attention, the timeline "many generations down the road" had been very quickly erased by mounting scientific evidence as well as more and more common real-world occurrences. We were seeing the effects *now*. Or at least the most vulnerable among us were.

These days, we seem to have new information almost monthly, and the gist of that new information can be summed up thus: it is worse than we thought, and it is happening faster than we predicted. Our formerly lengthy timeline has collapsed into urgency.

And what has the US done with this dawning knowledge? During the last two decades, the US has increased our carbon emissions by 7% per capita. In that same time, the UK has *reduced* their per capita emissions by 1%, Germany by 4%, Sweden by 15%, and Denmark by 19%.[6] While this level of reduction isn't nearly enough, we are seeing other countries with a similar level of de-

---

[5] That said, the first speculative mention of harmful warming of the atmosphere due to carbon emissions was apparently in a March 1912 issue of *Popular Mechanics* in an article titled, "Remarkable Weather of 1911: The Effect of the Combustion of Coal on the Climate—What Scientists Predict for the Future," by Frank Molena.

[6] www.theguardian.com/environment/datablog/2009/sep/02/carbon-emissions-per-person-capita.

velopment starting to reverse the trend. Not so here. We seem bound and determined to keep heading straight for the cliff, even as many of us can feel our weight shifting and the long fall starting.

This is just willful ignorance on our part in the US. And it is being perpetrated by politicians (who are either still arguing about whether climate change is real, or too far in the pockets of the fossil fuel industry to do anything without fear of losing their power, or, in the case of climate advocates, in too small of a minority to be effective); by businesses (many of whom rely on cheap fossil fuels to make a profit); and by average citizens (who are either merrily waltzing along in the comforts and routines of the relatively cushy American life that is normal here, or are caught in a vice grip of culture, economics, and other necessities and making themselves more than a little crazy not being able to act on what they know is ethically right and scientifically proven).

All of that adds up to a relationship status between America and fossil fuels perhaps best captured by a phrase from Facebook: *It's complicated.*

Rethinking Sustainability in Four Dimensions

Complicated indeed. The crisis we are facing has many aspects. One of the trickiest things is that you can't just solve many of our ecological problems directly or in isolation from a whole system that surrounds them. While the ecological realities are the most obvious, most tangible manifestation of the crisis, they are actually the end game of a whole series of causal pieces, and not where things start.

Let me explain. Since 2007, I have been working regularly with a curriculum developed by an organization called the Global Ecovillage Network (GEN). GEN is exactly what it sounds like: an international network of people living in and learning from ecovillage projects all over the world. In 1998, the educators among GEN started to notice patterns in what was being talked about. It seemed that no matter what political, socio-economic. and cultural context an ecovillage was being formed in, when they were really committed deeply to sustainability, the same questions and areas for consideration seemed to emerge during the process of developing and maturing that project.

By allowing that conversation to guide them, they were able to distill (over a multi-year process) a curriculum that identified four areas (or "dimensions" in the GEN lingo) of sustainability: ecological, economic, social, and worldview. In 2005, they released the first full iteration of their Gaia Education curriculum, which was later adopted by the United Nations as a "significant contribution" to sustainability.

Here's a brief description of each dimension.

- **Worldview:** our worldview is the fundamental lens through which we see everything: how we relate philosophically to ourselves, other beings, and the world. Some worldviews are secular and some are spiritual, but everyone has one. Our worldview includes how we relate to personal growth work. Our worldview drives everything else, and yet it is the most overlooked aspect of working toward real sustainability.

- **Social:** the social dimension includes how we share (or don't), cooperate (or don't), resolve conflicts (or don't), and make decisions (or don't). It includes interpersonal dynamics as well as broad societal structures and cultural norms around race, class, and gender. The social dimension is a *relational* expression of our worldview, describing us in interaction with other living beings.

- **Economic:** economics are actually a subset of social relationships, but are important enough in our current crisis of unsustainability to warrant their own dimension. Economics is how we get our tangible needs met, what exchange looks like, and what values we empower with our time, money, and energy. Economics is an *active* principle of our worldview—economics are resources and needs in motion with each other.

- **Ecological:** the ecological dimension is the most visible of the four dimensions, the one we can literally touch, and yet it is really the accumulated outcome of the previous three dimensions. It is both a very coarse and a very concrete expression of our values. Ecological decisions are our worldview expressed in how we use resources and caretake the physical environment, and they are filtered through (and largely determined by) social and economic relationships. The ecological dimension is a *tangible* expression of our worldview.

Worldview is the place where everything starts:[7] our ecological practices are the result of our worldview, and the social and economic systems that it generates. What you value, what you love (and even hold sacred, for those whose worldview takes on a spiritual flavor), these things determine what you are willing to act on behalf of. Worldview determines how you relate to other people, how you spend and make your money, and whether money is even the way you choose to get your needs met in the first place. All of this is true at the collective or cultural level, as well as at the individual level.

Trying to address ecological issues without paying significant attention to the worldview that is driving those issues (and the social and economic systems that act as translation filters between the worldview and ecological dimensions) is swimming upstream. And yet that is almost always how we approach ecological issues.

For instance, let's take the now iconic solar panel array, a very fine and

---

[7] Although, as Joanna Macy points out, our physical surroundings also have a way of shaping our worldview, and thus this whole model is a cyclical and iterative one. I think she is right about this, and so it is not quite as linear as I describe here. What I am focused on however is ecological *practices*, and I believe strongly that those are more an effect of the other three dimensions than deterministic of them: thus my characterization.

easy-to-understand contribution to carbon footprint reduction. A number of my friends who have tried to put solar panels on their houses have bumped into the economic barriers (they are still expensive, especially if you need to pay for them upfront, whereas coal is cheap…in part because we subsidize fossil fuel companies); they have bumped into social barriers (the neighbors freaking out about aesthetics and property values); and they have bumped into worldview barriers (often expressed as neighborhood association agreements that privilege certain lifestyle choices over others, policies of the local power companies that seem designed to discourage green power, or simply blank stares of the people that need to be brought on board).

There are parallels to this personal level of challenge at every other level, from the scale of our families, to our local municipalities, all the way up to the global system. As Naomi Klein says, in *This Changes Everything*, the worldview is a key piece of what needs to change, and I read her to say that it might even be the first and foremost piece if we are to get a real handle on climate change:

> The challenge…is not simply that we need to spend a lot of money and change a lot of policies; it's that we need to think differently, radically differently, for those changes to be remotely possible. Right now, the triumph of market logic with its ethos of domination and fierce competition, is paralyzing almost all serious efforts to respond to climate change. …For any of this to change, a worldview will need to rise to the fore that sees nature, other nations, and our own neighbors not as adversaries, but as partners in a grand project of mutual reinvention.[8]

Can you hear all four dimensions and how they relate in this quote? A worldview is needed that can drive how we relate differently to our neighbors and other nations (the social dimension). And our economic system, based on a competitive and profit-driven worldview (what she calls "market logic" here and expands on quite a bit elsewhere in the book) is leading to an inability to address an ecological crisis of growing magnitude. Thus, we can't just cut to the chase even globally and say, "Let's throw up a bunch of solar panels" and expect that to go smoothly (no matter how much of a no-brainer that might look to many of us).

Bringing it back down to the personal level for a moment, many of us know just how challenging becoming more ecologically responsible can be without significant support. In order for a post-carbon reality to come easily, we have to dismantle and reinvent this whole, multi-dimensional system, and it is my primary assertion in this book that community is a key element in that reinvention process, because community provides that support.

This Changes Everything is, I believe, the most important book that was published in 2014. Klein does a remarkable job of seeing and articulating the

---

[8] Naomi Klein, *This Changes Everything* (New York: Simon and Schuster, 2014) p. 23.

connections between these four dimensions, and she does it on the scale of national and international policy. The book you are reading is an attempt to do something similar on a personal, community, and village scale, because the power of a place like Dancing Rabbit is that it is one small-scale version of the exact project of reinvention that Klein is talking about.

One more important piece of context to be aware of in reading this book is Joanna Macy's work on social movements.[9] Macy says that every successful social movement has involved three types of activism:

1. Holding actions: basically, stopping more bad things from happening. This includes protests, civil disobedience, petitions, boycotts, and legal actions. If you have political power, it might include things like President Obama's halting of new leases on public lands for fossil fuel exploitation. None of these alone solve the problem, and most of them are temporary, but they do two things: they buy time, and they draw attention to the issue because holding actions are almost always acts that are outside of the norms of polite behavior or business as usual, and therefore draw attention.

   I love holding actions, very much believe that we need them, and regularly participate in them myself. However, they are not the focus of this book. I'm addressing here the second two parts of Macy's model, but feel it is very important to acknowledge holding actions as being just as much a part of what needs to be happening right now.

2. Systems change: changing how we act within the current system, changing how the system is fundamentally set up, and/or embodying an entirely new system. This book offers some options within each of these, but fundamentally encourages the third option, embodying a new system (from the personal level all the way up to international systems) as the deepest, long-term fix.

   There are two levels to this in this book: one is advocating for our creating holistic systems *within* intentional communities. The other is systems reform at the level of economic and legal reformation. I will be laying out a series of concrete proposals that would radically alter the regulatory and economic context that intentional communities find themselves operating within, something that would increase the rate of social change and community development considerably.

3. Worldview changes: reinventing our values and fundamental relationship to ourselves and others, including consciousness work. This is foundational for even getting started on real social change: we

---

[9] While Macy has written about this in many places, a great reference is the book *World as Lover, World as Self*, with a terrific forward by Thich Nhat Hanh, published in 1991 by Parallax Press.

have to re-vision where we are headed and what we want. We simply can't embody a new system when we are operating out of old consciousness.

I will talk a lot about worldview changes in this book. It is a central premise of all my work in the world that cooperative living both requires major shifts in how we see the world, and is an excellent training ground for those shifts.

Macy points out that not every person is going to participate in all three of these approaches, and that is perfectly fine. As an overall movement, however, we can't prosper and really progress without all three of these happening: we need to change our consciousness, and buy time, and use that time to create new systems embodying fundamentally different values, techniques, and technologies.

The changes we need to make in our systems are not really possible without the worldview work. Whatever changes we make need to come from a place of deeply understanding the implications of what we are proposing, and having a clear picture in our minds of where we are headed. This new worldview is the north star for guiding cultural and social change, and I see intentional communities as playing a critical role in those changes. The intentional communities movement needs to move beyond being a bunch of projects scattered across the continent, and into really leading some pieces of bigger social change. And to do so, all three of Macy's aspects of successful social movements will need to be in play.

Taking Apart Ecological Sustainability

An essential question of the ecological dimension is how to reduce our resource usage and our emissions. If our goal is to be living a high quality of life on 10% of the US average of both consumption and carbon emissions, we are going to need some serious tools to get that done. Anything less isn't sustainable.

That said, I don't mean to imply that if you can't make 10% next week, you shouldn't even try. One of the big ego games[10] we can get into with making ecological changes is mistaking partial progress for failure. Some of us don't think it is worth pursuing unless we can get to the ultimate goal right away. And yet, for almost all of us, gradual change is really the only route available to us.

It takes time to analyze our lives and make the right changes, and it takes time to develop new routines. If you can reduce your consumption and emissions by 20% this year, that's a huge win, *so long as you don't rest on that progress next year*.

---

[10] I talked about this and other ego games activists get caught up in in my first book *Passion as Big as a Planet*, in chapter 9 (Lulu Press, 2007).

Over the past two decades, I've lived in multiple different contexts: urban and rural, in a full-on ecovillage and in a regular house, with others and alone. In that time, I've been consistently tracking my personal ecological footprint,[11] and the results have been very interesting.

What I've found (anecdotally and with my one lone data point, so take this however seriously you think it deserves) is that it is not that hard to bring your overall eco footprint down to 70% or even 60% of the American average. (Partly this is because the American average is, frankly, appalling; but it IS the default, and most of us need some attention to not just going along with the crowd.)

Getting down to 40–50% of the US average is also possible, even living alone in a regular house. It's harder work and takes a lot of attention, but it can certainly be done, and I know many people who have pulled this off.

The last bit, however, is a bugger. Actually getting down to the 10% mark is very challenging, and the only places I've been able to get into that ballpark are in intentional communities with some real attention on sustainability. I still need to be conscientious of what I'm doing, but the whole environment is set up with the goal of seriously reducing our ecological impact and that makes everything much, much easier. In that context, we can, for instance: share cars and make meals together; have social support for thinking through ecological challenges, and witness role models all around us who bring new ideas to us; grow food in ways that are ecologically appropriate for that place, often producing food that is both local *and* organic.

Beyond my anecdotal sense of things, there have been a number of communities that have documented their gains, and I will share those statistics throughout this book. One group of those communities consists of the Boulder, Colorado co-ops. Keying off the average Colorado consumption levels,[12] here's where they rest in three areas: they use one third of the water, one third of the natural gas, and one quarter of the electricity. In a letter to the Boulder City Council,[13] engineer and researcher Jordan Mann and Boulder Housing Coalition Executive Director Lincoln Miller note:

---

[11] In the early years, I used a cool website that was designed for junior high kids, associated with a program called Eco-Voyageurs, but unfortunately it no longer exists. Once that went defunct, I switched to using the Stanford University one that seems, unlike most of them, to at least take into account more common practices that happen in intentional communities.

[12] I am mostly talking about communities' resource usage compared to the US average in this book, and this data set is discussed in terms of Colorado usage. Some quick research indicates that Colorado in general is a higher than average consumption state for water—about 20 gallons of water per day per person for domestic usage according to data on www.csgwest.org/policy/WesternWaterUsage.aspx—and is ranked 34th among states for use of overall energy, meaning it consumes less than the average of combined energy sources.

[13] The letter excerpted is from Feb. 10, 2015. Data was collected over a one year period from six Boulder cooperative houses: Radish, PickleBric, Masala, North Haven, Chrysalis, and The Beet. Thanks to Lincoln for sharing this with me.

Heating a 3,000 square foot home will use a similar amount of gas whether there is one person or 10 people living there. I had expected that other resource use such as electricity and water consumption would correlate more directly with the number of occupants (these co-ops range from eight residents up to 26 residents, with the median somewhere around 12 residents). What I found was that even per capita electricity and water usage are significantly lower in cooperatives.

Jordan also translated their work into carbon emissions data, which is even more relevant for our purposes here:

If all of us in Boulder used the same amount of energy per person as the co-op crowd, we would prevent over 125,000 tons of CO_2 from going into the atmosphere every year. Given Boulder's current electricity generation mix where 56% of our electricity comes from coal, the amount of coal that we would prevent from being burned could fill a coal train five miles long, about the length of the Boulder Creek path. On a per capita basis in the context of household energy use, the housing co-ops are close to meeting the city of Boulder's recently adopted climate commitment for 2050 (an 80% reduction in CO_2 emissions). Furthermore we've done it without changing our electricity supply, and in many cases without having the ability to significantly invest in the buildings we occupy. These emissions reductions have come not with significant financial costs, but with enormous, immediate, per capita savings.

Jordan and Lincoln's last point is especially interesting to me, because one of the frequent claims that critics of ecological lifestyle choices make is that it is far more expensive to do the right thing. Co-ops are generally not occupied by wealthy people—in fact urban co-ops are often home to students, activists, and artists as their main population draws, none of whom tend to be making high incomes. What co-ops demonstrate in part is that living a high quality, socially connected, ecologically sound life is possible for a range of income levels, if cooperation is used as a main tool for constructing that life.

The list is long of all the ways living cooperatively makes it easier to also live ecologically. I'll get into some more of the specifics in Chapter 2 where I talk more about Dancing Rabbit Ecovillage.

If you carefully take apart the last couple pages, the four dimensions all come to life. The worldview that the system is built on (our goals and the motivations for them), the cultural context you are in (the presence of peer support and willingness to cooperate so we can share resources), and the economic system we are in (what we have to do to get our needs met and thrive) all make a huge difference to how easy it is to live sustainably.

This is why just focusing on solar panels doesn't work as a full strategy. For a look at what that full strategy can look like, come back to the cornfields of Missouri with me in the next chapter. But first, one more quick note about why communities have something unique to offer in our discovery process for climate solutions.

Community as Experiential Laboratory

The appeal and potential of intentional communities lie largely in one of their fundamental characteristics: they are miniature social laboratories where we can try stuff out that is different—sometimes radically different—than the mainstream. Over the history of the communities movement, these social laboratories have been used to develop and/or hone a wide range of interesting tools. I have hopes that this inherent trait of communities can be leveraged ever more powerfully for engaging in what many have appropriately named "de-growth"—moving from a paradigm of perpetual growth and high consumerism to a cultural norm of lifestyles that dwell *within* the natural (and implacably firm) limits of the planet.

Dr. Joshua Lockyer, speaking to fellow social scientists, says this about ecovillages:

> For social scientists, these "utopian" communities serve as natural laboratories where deliberate design for sustainability is the starting point, and where ongoing attention to resource use and effective environmental stewardship shape the cultural context for human behavior, as manifested in explicitly stated community norms, rules, and ritual activities. Collaboration and engagement on the part of scholar-activists allow our skills of critical analysis and our desire to identify what does and does not work in the transition to resilient, sustainable societies to converge in synergistic ways with the interests of those we study.[14]

Having social scientists to document what we do is great because that adds legitimacy to the communities movement and provides us with information that helps us to be diligent about making sure what we are doing really is better. And yet intentional communities, it turns out, are very good at innovation, whether anyone is paying attention or not.

Examples range from the start of Habitat for Humanity[15] to car sharing[16] to a form of polyamory[17] to consensus decision-making[18] to lesser known but

---

[14] Dr. Lockyer is at Arkansas Tech University. Quote from a forthcoming article in the *Journal of Political Ecology*.

[15] This model was pioneered in Koinonia Community in Georgia, founded in 1942 as the first fully racially integrated town in the US.

[16] Done by many income sharing communities before it became popularized by urban programs like Zip Car.

[17] Kerista Community in California coined the term "polyfidelity" to describe integrity- and communication-based relationships with multiple partners, and to distinguish this practice from simply sleeping around or "swinging."

[18] Developed first by a number of indigenous tribes, and also by the Quakers (both of whom could be seen as intentional communities, or not, depending on your definition), and then spread widely through both the intentional communities and radical activist movements

still potent examples like Feedback Learning[19] and the ZEGG Forum.[20] And many natural building techniques were developed and studied in a community context (think Earthships) and then those examples later used to help change laws in places with more restrictive building codes, opening the door for wider dissemination of these techniques. All of these, in fact, are examples of things pioneered in the "safe bubble" of intentional communities before spreading out to wider cultural contexts.[21]

So, communities incubate a lot of interesting stuff. And every intentional community is experimental to some extent: all communities in the US are attempting something cooperative within the context of a highly competitive culture. (See Chapter 5 for more on that topic.) So community is always doing something different, something with no well-worn paths to follow, and that generally leads to its being a highly creative environment.

While that can be daunting, it is also very exciting. Trying out new stuff is not only encouraged, it is also essential to at least some extent, to create the fabric of real community in America today. Sure, some groups are a more radical departure from the mainstream (and therefore have a greater need for creativity), but all of them afford an opportunity for reinvention that is very much in line with Klein's imperative for making a new, post-carbon world.

This makes community a powerful place to be as the world is changing around us, and demanding we change, too. Banding together to navigate those changes means both amplifying our individual creativity (increasing our chances of bringing into being a viable new world in the process), and simultaneously offering a significantly safer haven to operate from as the world changes around us.

There's another reason community is a powerful tool for working on climate change: peer pressure. George Marshall has a fascinating chapter called *The Jury of Our Peers* in his book[22] on why we aren't dealing with climate change. In it, he details a whole host of ways in which the inaction of those around us leads to us being less likely to act ourselves, regardless of what

---

where a more secularized version of consensus now flourishes.

[19] Developed by Ganas Community on Staten Island in New York, this method is about helping people learn to give and receive accurate, non-dramatic feedback, and work through the common emotional reactivity in that process.

[20] A type of witnessed issues processing work that is often likened to "psychodrama" for its use of acting out parts of our own psyche for the purpose of psychological growth and healing.

[21] There are also more amusing examples, that have spread a lot further: the sugar waffle ice cream cone and automatic bowling pin reset are both inventions claimed by Mary's City of David, a community in Benton Harbor, Michigan. This community also once played an exhibition basketball game against the Harlem Globetrotters, and is the third oldest Christian community in the US, according to their website. If the creativity of just one intentional community can produce this range of wonders, surely a whole movement of us can make a dent in this climate thing.

[22] George Marshall, *Don't Even Think About It: Why Our Brains Are Wired to Ignore Climate Change* (London: Bloombury Publishers, 2014).

we personally believe to be right or feel moved to do, and regardless of the urgency of what is in front of us.

The opposite is true as well: make it cool to take climate change seriously, surround yourself with people who are acting, and you are far more likely to act. Community is an activist tool because of *psychology*, not only because of economies of scale. We are not only more powerful together — we can also be more aligned with our values when we surround ourselves with others who will be a positive force in keeping us honest.

Chapter 2: Limiting the Damage:
Community as a Tool to Reduce Carbon Footprints

Community often forms as a response to duress and crisis, but it can also be formed deliberately. And of course, some places in the world never lost community as a fundamental way of organizing getting their needs met.

The Mother of All Sustainability Skills

The basic advantage that intentional communities have over individual efforts is the ability to leverage sharing and cooperation as main tools for becoming more ecological. In my 2013 TEDx talk,[23] I dubbed cooperation the "Mother of All Sustainability Skills." Note that I frame it as a *skill*. Skills are learnable, and require regular practice to get (and stay) good at them. Cooperation is not a skill we are taught very much in our American education system, something I will talk more about in Chapter 5. But for now, the key point I want to make is that the members of almost any intentional community endeavor are going to have a lower ecological and carbon footprint almost automatically than their go-it-alone neighbors because all communities share and cooperate to some extent.

While most communities do not collect statistics on their ecological impact, some do. The Boulder Co-ops that I cited in the last chapter are one example. Another is EcoVillage at Ithaca, in Ithaca, New York.

From EcoVillage at Ithaca's website:

> PhD student Jesse Sherry from Rutgers University found that the ecological footprint of EcoVillage Ithaca residents is 70% less than typical Americans. This means that people in our community use only about 30% of the total resources needed for travel, heat, electricity, food, water and waste.

What's interesting to me about the two examples we have so far (the Co-ops and EcoVillage at Ithaca) is that they are very different models of intentional communities, but both are seeing significant gains ecologically. The Boulder Co-ops get a lot of their gains by living in smaller spaces per person,

---

[23] www.youtube.com/watch?v=BS8YeDKKBcU. The talk was done at Carleton College in Northfield, Minnesota on October 12, 2013.

generally living a less consumptive life, and are a more affordable housing option for people in Boulder. That life, though, is not necessarily appealing to a lot of people.

EcoVillage at Ithaca has different appeal: they combine ecovillage thinking with the cohousing model,[24] which is a much more "normal looking" way of living for Americans: each household has their own private spaces in addition to a common house and other common facilities that are shared. They are not necessarily any cheaper than other similar housing in the area, so their appeal is to a different crowd.

Cohousing has done a lot for expanding the appeal of intentional communities within the US, and while it is often not as potent an ecological tool as more communal types of community are, EcoVillage at Ithaca is a great example of a group which has used the basic framework of cohousing as part of a creative package that leads to significantly reduced ecological footprints.

And then there is Dancing Rabbit.

Anecdotally (but based on having visited almost 100 communities in North America with an eye toward analyzing their ecological approach), I think Dancing Rabbit is doing the best of any larger community (which I am calling over 40 people in year-'round residence) in the US in terms of overall ecological sustainability. I know of smaller groups that are probably doing better (Sandhill Farm and the Possibility Alliance, both also in northeastern Missouri, come to mind, though they haven't as far as I know collected statistics). However, when we start talking about cultural transformation, the ability to scale up is important. And that's always been Dancing Rabbit's intention.

It's also the community that I know the best, so it is easy for me to paint this picture for you. So let's look behind the curtain at what this successful community is doing, and get a glimpse into our potential collective future.

Case Study One: Dancing Rabbit Ecovillage

I first visited DR in the spring of 1998 (the spring after the founders bought a piece of rough land in rural Missouri that had most recently been an abandoned pig farm). What ensued was a very slow-motion courting process with the community: visiting, living there for short stints, going away again to try to form community somewhere else, visiting again, and then finally in 2008 moving back and staying for over eight years.

I got to see a community go from the visionary stage, with Tony Sirna and Cecil Scheib saying to a group of us the first time I toured the community, "Someday a whole village will be here!," to being myself a central community

---

[24] Cohousing comes to us from Denmark, and was originally conceptualized and developed by an architect and psychologist, Jan Gudmand-Hoyer, who thought that we could do better at housing ourselves, both in terms of social connection and sustainability. Cohousing was brought to the US by architects Chuck Durrett and Katie McCamant.

member of that village and its nonprofit, living and breathing the reality of sustainability.

The founders did a lot of things right. Bucking conventional wisdom (or perhaps more fairly, stereotypes) these just-graduated-from-college smart young folks started from a place of relative humility and sought out a pre-existing community to be a mentor for them. That community, Sandhill Farm, had been started in 1974 by a group that included the Fellowship for Intentional Community's primary staffer for several decades, Laird Schaub. Laird is an expert in social dynamics, and between the basic sensibility of our founders, Laird's wise counsel, and the lived experience of others at Sandhill, Dancing Rabbit understood early on that the social dimension was incredibly important.[25]

The founders also set some very high bars on the ecological front for people joining. Six ecological covenants form the central agreements people make with each other and the community when they join. Here's the current iteration of those:

1. Dancing Rabbit members will not use personal motorized vehicles, or store them on Dancing Rabbit property.

2. At Dancing Rabbit, fossil fuels will not be applied to the following uses: powering vehicles, space-heating and -cooling, refrigeration, and heating domestic water.

3. All gardening, landscaping, horticulture, silviculture, and agriculture conducted on Dancing Rabbit property must conform to the standards as set by OCIA for organic procedures and processing. In addition, no petrochemical biocides may be used or stored on DR property for household or other purposes.

4. All electricity produced at Dancing Rabbit shall be from sustainable sources. Any electricity imported from off-site shall be balanced by Dancing Rabbit exporting enough on-site, sustainably generated electricity, to offset the imported electricity.

5. Lumber used for construction at Dancing Rabbit shall be either reused/reclaimed, locally harvested, or certified as sustainably harvested.

6. Waste disposal systems at Dancing Rabbit shall reclaim organic and recyclable materials.

That's a lot of things that the community regulates, but note as well how much they *don't* regulate. They say nothing about dietary choices, the square footage of homes, use of plastic or electronics...all of which are certainly

---

[25] In fact, it is the most common place of failure in trying to have viable community. Most groups that fail do so because of a breakdown in conflict resolution skills, lack of facilitation skills to keep decision-making moving along in a solid way, or a general lack of understanding of the immense cultural shift they are taking on in moving from a competitive to a cooperative framework.

ecologically impactful. The DR founders made a deliberate choice to regulate a handful of things that they believed were both very impactful on a person's (and therefore a community's) ecological footprint, and could also be relatively easily tracked, but were less likely to lead to neighbors policing each other's behavior in an invasive way.

A policing environment is a common downfall of many well-intentioned sustainability projects: the holier-than-thou are, frankly, notoriously hard to be around for any length of time, let alone live with every day.

The founders had good discernment about what to regulate and not. For example, hiding the existence of a personal car on the property is hard enough that people don't try. Thus, from a "let's avoid policing" standpoint, banning personal car usage is relatively safe. On the other hand, smuggling a bag of Cheetos and a burger into the community would be sorely tempting (and a heck of a lot easier to get away with) if there were rules to be broken about meat or junk food consumption, and suspicions that someone is violating a rule can lead to all kinds of bad feelings.

I believe this particular filter of the DR founders has served the community well over the years. The danger is that people will conform with just this relatively limited list of restrictions and then have otherwise horrible practices, leading to very spotty gains in ecological progress. However, it turns out that happens only up to a point, and no further, because of the nature of consciousness.

DR members rely on people's ability to self-sort. They trust that people will apply to live in a place like DR only if they have a generally high level of consciousness around ecological practices. The high standards of the covenants help create a kind of litmus test for that. Frankly, if an American is willing to pry their hands off their personal car keys (one of the most amazing processes of consciousness shift you'll ever see) they are probably willing to do a lot of things, whether someone is standing over them demanding it or not. And to a large extent, that works at Dancing Rabbit.

So what has the impact been of Dancing Rabbit's set-up? Here are the 2015 statistics[26] expressed as the percentage of average American consumption:

- 19% of water, over half from rainwater catchment (8.5% of municipal-source water)

- 13% of landfill waste, while doing higher than average recycling

- 14% of the US average of electricity used, including most of their business activities, and a net exporter of solar power onto the grid

- 5% of propane/natural gas

- 6% of fuel for vehicles, owning 7% of the cars.

---

[26] The statistics come from anthropologist Brooke Jones, who did her Master's Thesis work on Dancing Rabbit's ecological practices, and has returned to continue collecting data, including these numbers from 2015.

These numbers put Dancing Rabbit right in the ballpark of our magic 10% mark in the areas measured. Thus we have a very concrete example that shows that sustainable is possible in these areas, and that community is a viable pathway to a low consumption future.

Two sets of data not included above are food and buildings. Both of these categories have proven complicated to measure. Where the community car sharing program makes it relatively easy to track miles driven in a year, the many sources of food community members rely on makes food footprints very hard to accurately measure. Same goes with buildings: a lot of factors go into determining the ecological and/or carbon footprint of a building (including the materials used, the distance they were shipped, the size of the building, and use of things like passive solar techniques…and then there is variation in how different renters or owners might occupy that building). What that means is that it is hard to get really good numbers, especially on a low research budget.

Here's what we do know about Rabbit building and food practices, all of which bode pretty well for them having a noticeably lower than average footprint in both areas. Rabbits have, on average, about 30% of the personal space of most Americans, and, since 80% of the carbon emissions in the life of a building come from occupying it (largely heating and cooling), the square footage is considered to be the best predictor of carbon footprint of a building.[27]

Dancing Rabbit has one of the highest concentrations of natural buildings in the midwest, including a number of strawbale and cob buildings, which are built using clay from their own property, straw from about 20 miles away, and sand from a local quarry. The ecological covenants also limit what wood can be used in construction to reclaimed lumber, locally sustainably harvested, and certified sustainable lumber. Most buildings also make use of passive solar and other green design techniques. Finally, none of them are heated with fossil fuels.[28]

In terms of food, meat eaters at Dancing Rabbit appear to consume less than the American average, with a portion of the meat being produced within walking distance of where it is consumed; similarly most people get a high percentage of their dairy from an organic farm just a few miles away. And, predictably, there are people who eat little or no meat and dairy. Most people

---

[27] Jordan Palmeri, *A Life Cycle Approach to Prioritizing Methods of Preventing Waste from the Residential Construction Sector in the State of Oregon*, 2010, www.deq.state.or.us/lq/pubs/docs/sw/ResidentialBldgLCAExecSummary.pdf.

[28] It is possible that last statement is not entirely accurate. I will talk later about the decision to go "on grid" for a good portion of the community's electricity needs, while being a net exporter of electricity, a commitment the community has kept. However, that does mean that sometimes someone will be running an electric heater at night when the solar panels do not produce power, and therefore will be pulling some coal-produced electricity. While the net export commitment makes this fine for many people, there is not a claim on Dancing Rabbit's part to be "pure" in terms of their electric consumption.

either have their own gardens or try to get produce from farmers who live in the community, or from two of the other nearby intentional communities (one less than a mile away and the other a whole three miles away).

So we know Dancing Rabbit's food and housing practices are not standard American practices, and are likely to produce lower carbon emissions, but we don't have the slick statistics on the community with exact percentages the way we do in those other areas.

As the statistics above show, while the community does not choose to regulate water usage, it is still using a fraction of an average American's water per capita. Same with the number of miles driven—no rule prohibits being a gas hog, but the combination of community systems discouraging commuter lifestyles and casual car usage and the high degree of consciousness among people who join the community adds up to a very strong showing in the fuel conservation category.

Witness also that the farmers growing organic food on the property have a lot of local buyers for their products, even though the community doesn't say you have to eat locally and organically. Thus, the idea that people who are willing to live with a strong batch of regulations are *also* likely to have consciousness beyond those particular regulated areas seems to be true at Dancing Rabbit.

Obviously resource use reduction and carbon footprint reduction are not identical, but they are very closely related. Dancing Rabbit also engages in a number of activities that positively impact their carbon footprint (such as having planted about 15,000 trees over the years). Thus, when we think about solutions to climate change, we need to look not only at reducing negative impacts, but also at increasing our positive ones, and DR deserves credit for working both ends of that equation.

Dancing Rabbit is an excellent example of what a group can do with a very strong focus on the social and ecological dimensions, and with strong enough worldview articulation early on.[29] They also made some very good decisions early on that set up their members to be able to operate with only one foot in the wider, unsustainable economy (though my sense is that the economic dimension strengths of DR have evolved over time, not as carefully crafted by the founders as the social and ecological dimensions were). The choices to locate in a place with a low cost of living, to de-emphasize car culture and materialism, and to strongly emphasize resource sharing and casual labor swaps have led to the community being relatively economically accessible (especially for people who are either able-bodied or have strong skills that can be sold on the internet).

Another economic feature of Dancing Rabbit took longer to catch on but

---

[29] In addition to the ecological covenants, Dancing Rabbit has sustainability guidelines that are more philosophical in nature and provide significant food for thought for members: www. dancingrabbit.org/about-dancing-rabbit-ecovillage/vision/sustainability-guidelines.

now colors the life of the community very strongly: the ELM system. ELM stands for "exchange local money" and is one of the most used local (or complementary or alternative, depending on what language you prefer) currency systems in the world. As far as we know, DR is the only place in the world where someone can pay for their food, housing, transportation, and utilities using entirely a local currency. Most local currency programs have found that the biggest barrier to being viable is people not being able to pay for some basic service with it. At DR, you can pay for nearly all of your basics with it. Thus, the ELM system has a very high annual per capita use rate: 10,840 ELMs are exchanged per year per person on average.[30]

A couple other important features of Dancing Rabbit relate both to its carbon footprint and to its viability as a community socially. Those are the option of subgroups (or sub-communities[31]) forming for various purposes, and a particular form of subgroups, the eating co-ops. I characterize Dancing Rabbit as a village whose main structure is a series of overlapping cooperatives. These cooperatives give people the option of being part of deeper resource, income, and labor sharing, or choosing to be more independent.

So you can be part, for instance, of the shower co-op at the Common House, or you can construct your own shower facilities elsewhere. Same with landline phone service, internet access, grid-tied electrical service, and the humanure system, all of which are formal co-ops anyone in the community can join or pass on. Co-ops have also formed around agriculture (e.g., the goat and chicken co-op) as well any number of eating scenes hosted in structures (including both standard-looking kitchens and "outdoor kitchens" that are seasonal) that have large enough kitchens that can accommodate daily cooking for eight to 30 people.

This makes Dancing Rabbit pretty unique: you can live in this community and live your life as communally as you want, or you can live there and share only a few resources with others (the Common House and land are required to share, and if you are going to drive a car, you need to be in the Dancing Rabbit Vehicle Co-op). One of the best things about that is that as your needs change, as they tend to do when people are in different life phases, you can stay within your same community and just change the amount of communal versus independent aspects of your life.

Most intentional communities are designed with more of a one-size-fits-all model—you either income share, or you don't; you cook and eat meals together, or you don't;[32] you have a shared electrical grid, or you don't. At

---

[30] Personal communication from the ELM system manager.

[31] So far, the longest running of the subcommunities was Skyhouse, an income sharing group within Dancing Rabbit that lasted for 16 years. These options are important because they give people in the village different economic, spiritual, and social options without the whole community having to get on board with deeper values alignment.

[32] By this I mean eating all your meals together—nearly every community has some meal sharing, though it is common in the less communal versions of community to have this

Dancing Rabbit, all of those are options, and you can try out different things over time…without losing your social support network by having to leave the community to do it.

Finally, Dancing Rabbit is a fascinating mix of how to relate to technology use. While the community relies heavily on email communication and other electronic systems (the car sharing system, bulk food ordering, local currency, and aspects of decision-making all require people to get on a computer with some regularity to be able to fully participate) there is a wide range of other relationships to technology.

Some people's homes look very similar to a standard middle-class American existence: running water, kitchen gadgets galore, electricity backed up by grid power so you have just as few days without power as anyone else in the wider neighborhood. And these homes were often built using power tools, sometimes even with heavy equipment to dig foundations and place beams.

Other homes are basically glorified bedrooms: tiny houses with no running water, and some even without electricity—these residents rely on the Common House or other cooperative infrastructure to get those needs met. Some were built with hand tools only (or very rare use of limited power tools) and lots of work-party muscle to get things done.

Most houses fall between these two extremes. And that's OK. One of the cool things about Dancing Rabbit is that those variations are all OK. While occasional tensions arise around these issues, for the most part I experience Dancing Rabbit as being both a relatively judgment-free zone about those choices,[33] and a place that deliberately celebrates the diversity of choices as legitimate expressions of sustainability.

Among other things, this can make it easier for people of various levels of financial means to make it work. It also helps with more diversity in able-bodiedness: if you need your water to come out of the tap (as opposed to hauling it), have some gadget for medical reasons, drive places instead of biking, or have a brick walkway leading up to your door, that's all fine. On the other hand, if you want to get by on $3,000 a year of income and do a lot of stuff yourself without investing in modern conveniences, that works, too.

---

be one meal a week, or a few meals a week. That is basically an independent eating scene community with some partial sharing. An advantage to being more of a full meal sharing community is having to build a lot less kitchen infrastructure, which is both expensive and resource intensive.

[33] I wish I could say this was common among people who take sustainability seriously, but I can't. And as our urgency around climate disruption rises, it can be very easy to slip further into frustration with other people's choices. While some Rabbits will tell you that they have felt judged (and I felt that sting at times myself) I'm making these comments and characterizations within the context of the wider culture, where judgment seems to be the *norm* among intellectuals and activists of all sorts, and even seems to happen within the communities movement between communities who think they have the "right" answers. I stand by the statement that DR is way above average in creating an open space for lots of options: yes, judgments happen at DR, but when they do, it stands out as being unusual…and THAT is unusual.

A Four-Dimension Analysis of Dancing Rabbit

I'm holding Dancing Rabbit up as the primary example in this book of a "Four-Dimension Community," one whose strengths derive in part from having engagement in all four areas the Global Ecovillage Network's curriculum says are necessary for deep sustainability. Here's a quick glance at ways I see the community doing well in these areas.

Worldview:

- The community started with a clear vision, and took the time to articulate not only the covenants but also the more philosophical and challenging questions of how to re-think our relationship to the planet, each other, and global ethics.

- The recognition of the need for personal growth work has grown steadily over the years at Dancing Rabbit, and the visitor program (designed to introduce people to what they would need to know and work with if they joined the community) has a workshop on inner sustainability.

- The community has rituals that help reinforce the culture change that is happening, corresponding to both the annual calendar and the weekly rhythm of the community. And while these rituals are not religious, the community derives a sense of bonding, stability, and connection from these that is absolutely worldview-changing.

- The community has used consensus all along, which directly undermines the "in it for myself" worldview of wider American culture.

- Similarly, having a strong commitment to not being a commuter culture is a big worldview shift for Americans. Cars represent so much of modern Americanism: independence and freedom, casual consumerism—and even have become a symbol of adulthood. To let go of our primary relationship with the car is a big deal.

- Direct contact with nature is a big feature of most people's lives. Much of the community's food is grown right on the land; no roads are paved within the community and most people get around on foot through woodsy walking paths; and people frequently take walks on the 280 acres of land (a chunk of which is designated as nature preserve). The natural world is a significant player in the community.

- DR practiced humility and a willingness to learn from other communities who had gone before them, a key element in their success. This humility continues in such things as having an EcoProgress Committee, and regularly bringing in new trainers of new techniques.

Social:

- Nonviolent conflict resolution is important at DR, and the community has put in place expectations, processes, support structures, and regular trainings to reinforce this.

- As noted above, consensus brings people into relationship with each other in a way that voting systems don't. The community also does regular training to build their skills in decision-making.
- There's a lot of collective fun created in the community—parties, float trips on nearby rivers, movie nights, telling of life stories, regular meal sharing, both planned and chance encounters at the swimming pond, and daily happy hour at the cooperatively run restaurant and B&B.
- Work parties get things done. Work is also a shared sphere, rather than an isolating one for many Rabbits.
- Systems support sharing: for instance, the online car sign-up is paired with time at the community's weekly coordination meeting to make for smooth sharing. Systems are also in place for the cleaning and maintenance of community assets (cars, the Common House, and the land) which helps with responsible management of the Commons.
- Dancing Rabbit's commitment to be a model and teach others means that thousands of people each year benefit from learning new skills and techniques, and being inspired to see that sustainability is indeed possible.

Economic:
- The ELM system has a large impact—the money created in the community is used to provide interest-free financing for community entities, helping members put some distance between themselves and the predatory banking system. It also encourages people to think in terms of spending locally and keeping their money circulating within the local economy.
- Extensive barter and casual labor-sharing mean reduced expenses and a more human-engaged way of getting needs met.
- The choice to locate in an inexpensive part of the country, while challenging in terms of lack of job opportunities, served to both reinforce the "not a commuter culture" ethic of the community, and made it more financially accessible for many people to join.
- No join fee means there is not an economic barrier to getting into the community.
- Collective buying power is put to work in many ways, including paying for the land, having access to equipment such as a big truck and a tractor, and even starting their own electric company to invest in a much bigger solar array than anyone could have done individually.
- The community has a very tight wage ratio (2:1) meaning that no one working for an official community entity can be making more than

twice what the lowest-paid person makes. This embodies economic justice and equity values.

- One of the best known businesses at Dancing Rabbit, the Milkweed Mercantile, recently went from being privately owned to being a cooperative.

Ecological:

- Talking ecological issues is normalized in the community allowing the problems in our world to be on the table, and therefore solvable with collective creativity.

- Meeting the ballpark 10% mark in resource consumption is a remarkable achievement; stay tuned for data on more categories.

- The most radical aspect of DR's ecological practices is the car co-op: four cars are shared by the full community, which has been as large as 65 adults in the last decade.

- Land stewardship is a big deal: the community has planted about 15,000 trees during its tenure on the land, and there are several committees that work on the community's relationship with the property (from long-term planning, to insuring buildings are placed and constructed in as nurturing a way as possible, to planting those trees and other land management tasks).

- The net export commitment with green electricity insures that the benefits of DR's cooperative lifestyle extend beyond the borders of the property.

- Not resting on its past achievements, many people at DR embody a lifelong learning ethic. One of the current manifestations of this is a partnership with Midwest Permaculture, where many DR residents are able to get holistic design training in permaculture to help improve the overall community practices as well as design better individual projects.

When I think of what the future might look like for all of us, living more sustainably, Dancing Rabbit features very large in my vision. This is a community that has pulled off some remarkable achievements, without governmental approval or support;[34] without the use of any fancy technology (beyond what is widely available, currently on the market); and with using learnable social skills such as deliberation, compassion, and cooperation as their main go-to's to figure things out. While this took strong intentionality, and this group was fortunate to be able to put together initial funding from members,

---

[34] The only governmental funding DR has utilized was a Department of Natural Resources grant to build a pond for erosion control, and Conservation Reserve Program funding for some of the land management. Both of these programs are ones that are very common in a lot of states.

friends, and families, there is nothing magical or non-replicable about what this community has done. In many ways, this was regular people with clear vision banding together for the benefit of us all.

Variations on the Theme of Low-Carbon Community

The Dancing Rabbit model is not the only way to create a low-carbon community. In fact, the word community means a lot of different things.

While I am mostly talking in this book about residential intentional communities (characterized by shared values and shared living space), community also means a variety of other things, including: sharing an identity (as in the queer community), living in the same town (geographical community), sharing a basic orientation in life (the conservative community), sharing an interest (the homeschooling community), sharing an experience (the Burner[35] community), or sharing a religion (the Catholic community). All of these are legitimate expression of community, which really implies getting your social needs met and often includes being economically connected and falling within a certain range of worldview commonality as well.

I want to highlight some examples of communities that are not embracing a full-on residential intentional community form, but are nonetheless using community as a tool for carbon reduction. This is my answer to a frequent criticism of the communities movement, "Not everyone is just going to move to the country and join a commune,[36] you know."

Here's a list of really interesting projects that use community to address climate change.

1. The Hoop

   The Hoop is a grassroots network of nomadic rewilders who live and travel with the seasons, living mostly on National Forest land throughout the Columbia Plateau and Great Basin bioregions in the northwest US. Bruno Seraphin at the University of Oregon has spent a couple summers and a few other shorter stints studying, living with, and sometimes traveling with the Hoopsters, and my information comes from him.

   Their central focus is to replant and tend wild food gardens and

---

[35] As in people who participate in Burning Man events.

[36] This is a good time to note how much that framing—which really IS the most common way it gets said to me—drives those of us who are in the movement a little crazy. First, not all communities are rural. In the current Communities Directory in fact, of communities that list a location, 26% are urban, 10% are suburban, and 11% are in a small town. That means only about half are rural. Second, "commune" means communities that share income, and while a small percentage of communities (16%) in the Directory do income sharing, most do not. Finally, we are all well aware that not everyone is going to embrace living with others. The US has a pretty low percentage of its overall population in fact who live in communities of this sort—Laird Schaub, the former long-time Executive Director of FIC puts it around .003% of the US population. Believe us, we get it!

bring them back into abundance. This has duel purposes. First, like any other gardeners, they are cultivating food for themselves, and the idea (and reality) is that when they come back around the next year to that place, there will be more abundance. Second, and more interesting for my purposes, they are working on recreating a more ecologically balanced and regenerative relationship with the natural world, and many are motivated by climate change.

The Hoopsters don't really have leaders as we would normally think of them, but the primary teacher who has helped create a movement of sorts is Finisia Medrano. Medrano in turn learned much of what she shares from the local indigenous people and their botanical traditions. The Planting Back website has this short bio of her: "Our community owes much to 'Tranny Granny' Finisia Medrano, infamous rewilder and author of 'Growing Up in Occupied America.' Finisia has spent years 'on the hoop' with her horses, gathering the traditional foods of the Great Basin. She has devoted her life to sharing hoop wisdom with others, and she has spent time in jail for acting on her beliefs." Medrano's nickname comes from another alternative culture life achievement: she is believed to have been the recipient of the first legal sex change surgery in California.

Hoopster worldview has some very relevant pieces for all of us. "Theirs is a philosophy of working with regenerative forces—not leave no trace, leave a beautiful trace," Bruno told me. The Hoopsters are both emulating the indigenous people from the region they occupy, with a close relationship to the land and deep respect for natural cycles, and at the same time professing a kind of attitude that is too single-minded to make for good coalition-building—bordering on holier-than-thou, in my reading of it—that Seraphin and I both find problematic. "Overall, they are taking bold steps to re-imagine some of our most deepseated assumptions about the way the world works, what a human being is, and what our relationships to the non-human should be. At same time, they are struggling to overcome assumptions and ways of being that serve to perpetuate colonialism, genocide, and environmental destruction. The Hoop, like any social movement, is shot through with contradictions."

2. Ashton Hayes, UK

Community-led solutions that do not require governmental buy-in are a terrific way to proceed when attempting to address climate change.[37] In 2006, the small English town of Ashton Hayes set their sights on becoming the first carbon neutral town in the UK, and in the

---

[37] And with the recent ascension of Donald Trump to power, it is more compelling than ever to see these local solutions in action: waiting on this government to get involved in the next four years is unlikely to yield much.

first year, reduced their collective carbon footprint by 20%. They've continued to make progress every year since then.[38]

One of the interesting things is seeing how that decision affected their relationships with each other, reinforcing the idea from our opening section that the social is not easily separable from the ecological. "Community cohesion has increased significantly since the carbon neutrality mission was adopted. One reason for this, resident Garry Charnock suggests, is that the carbon neutrality mission was created by and for the people in the town, without the influence or direction of politicians (who are only allowed to listen at meetings if they attend). There were never any community-wide mandates to contribute to the cause—just neighbors inspiring each other to make an effort here and there."[39]

As an intentional communities advocate, I find this model particularly compelling. In some ways, by bonding over this particular shared value, they have transformed themselves from a geographical community into an intentional community (a group that shares both values and place). This is a potent example of what happens when people embrace the concept of a Transition Town.[40] Sometimes, the unintended consequences turn out to be really positive ones!

The Transition US website defines their work in this way:

> The Transition Movement is comprised of vibrant, grassroots community initiatives that seek to build community resilience in the face of such challenges as peak oil, climate change, and the economic crisis. Transition Initiatives differentiate themselves from other sustainability and 'environmental' groups by seeking to mitigate these converging global crises by engaging their communities in home-grown, citizen-led education, action, and multi-stakeholder planning to increase local self reliance and resilience. They succeed by regeneratively using their local assets, innovating, networking, collaborating, replicating proven strategies, and respecting the deep patterns of nature and diverse cultures in their place. Transition Initiatives work with deliberation and good cheer to create a fulfilling and inspiring local way of life that can withstand the shocks of rapidly shifting global systems.

3. New Vistas

Mormonism is fundamentally a *millennialist* religion. That means that, prior to the rapture, Mormons anticipate a period (generally

---

[38] www.upworthy.com/this-little-town-decided-to-go-green-and-they-did-it-without-the-government?

[39] Ibid.

[40] Originally inspired by Rob Hopkins' book, *The Transition Handbook: from Oil Dependency to Local Resilience*, the movement has spread onto every continent.

thought to be 1,000 years—thus the term millennialist) of heaven being manifest on earth. This has lent a utopian flavor to various periods of Mormon history, though in recent years, it has drifted away from those roots. David Hall is a man who is bringing these roots back, with a distinctly modernistic flavor, in the form of the New Vistas project.

While Hall insists that the New Vistas project is not a "Mormon project" per se, he has also based the fundamentals on a handful of documents recorded by Joseph Smith, the founder of the church, and Smith himself attempted to bring communalism into the early church. Given that Smith bumped into the American hyper-independence tendency and couldn't get enough folks on board, it is probably wise that Hall has tried to put some distance between the church and his project. And yet, the project shares cultural and textual roots with the church, and there is something potentially powerful and definitely interesting about that.

New Vistas seeks to be a modern eco-utopia, with carefully designed cities of up to one million people living in housing and sharing buildings that would not be out of place in a *Jetsons* episode. Where the Hoopsters are going super low tech in their approach, and the citizens of Ashton-Hayes are building a grassroots movement from the ground up, New Vistas is very much about tech and design as tools to create optimal human environments for low-carbon living. And it is also all about scale, as in large-scale.

While this project is still on paper and not yet at the prototype phase it is worth mentioning here as an example of a project with a lot of money behind it,[41] and an attempt to move us out of hyper-independent worldviews through providing a large amount of physical comfort and ease of daily life, without all the carbon. Hall has a pretty unique vision in that the community businesses (rather than the residents) would income-share, with all profits going into a collective pool that would cover both the shareable business needs (such as marketing and accounting) and the needs of the community. Community members would mostly work in these businesses.

This has the potential to do an end-run around some of the stickier interpersonal dynamics of income sharing, while providing many of the benefits (including cost savings and ecological savings by being able to take advantage of massive-scale bulk buying and growing of food). It also has the potential to create some traditionally very bad dynamics in terms of a "company store" set-up, where people could get locked into working for businesses that could easily abuse this

---

[41] Hall's family money comes from the artificial diamond industry, and their main clients have been the mining industry. Hall no longer owns that business, having sold it a few years back to focus all of his attention, and his considerable wealth, on the New Vistas project.

situation. In fact, I think the biggest X-factor in this project is how the social dynamics will play out.[42]

Tools Communities Use (and You Can, Too)

A recent National Public Radio story[43] has been much on my mind as I've been writing. It highlighted a group of residents who bought the mobile home park they lived in when the owner decided to sell it. The residents had faced sudden loss of stability and of inexpensive housing. Since they bought it, they have slowly transformed it from a fairly impersonal neighborhood into a democratically run community. It's an example of how community can spontaneously erupt in unexpected places in response to a challenge, and how an economic stake in your home can lead to greater social connection and responsibility for each other.

What I like about this story is how it blurs the lines between intentional community and the wider culture. I find myself musing on the possibility that some day the phrase "intentional community" will draw blank stares for a different reason than it does today: because everyone will have an integrated sense of community. Someday, the version of community I advocate for might well be quaint and antiquated. And that's just fine with me.

How we get there is by both promoting the formation of a lot more formal intentional communities, and finding ways to bring community into our lives in a host of other ways. I see the edges of those movements someday meeting, and when that happens, we will have transformed our culture.

There are a lot of ways I see that second thing happening, and I'm going to highlight four of them here. These are cooperative tools you can employ right now wherever you live, and also represent important initiatives that help with the climate crisis.

Great Idea 1: Community-Based Agriculture

I have a particular soft spot in my heart for community gardens programs: my first real professional job was as the Program Director of Ann Arbor, Michigan's Project Grow Community Gardens, back in the early '90s. At the time, I had no real political analysis about food systems, nor was Ann Arbor a place that was really suffering from widespread food deserts.

---

[42] For the sake of transparency, I heard about this project first in mid-2016 and ended up doing a short-term contract with the project to help develop social systems. Because there were not yet actual people involved to work with (an essential element in the work I do!), I ended up not being able to do much for the project. Perhaps in 10 years when there are real people to work with, I'll have another shot at helping. As a project basically designed by engineers, it seems to me that the likelihood of the core social dynamics becoming a main focus is fairly low. Which is too bad.

[43] The story by Daniel Zwerdling on *All Things Considered*, called "When Residents Take Ownership, A Mobile Home Community Thrives," ran on December 27, 2016. The Northcountry Cooperative Foundation is the organization that has helped over 200 mobile home neighborhoods transform into resident-owned and -run cooperatives.

Since then, though, I've watched the spread of community gardens and similar ideas in much more deeply urbanized areas, and I've become considerably more politicized (partly through these stories). The racial and class divide in how we eat is one of the more distressing aspects of oppression for me, because it literally undermines the core strength and well-being of poor populations everywhere. It is low-level, daily violence, and kills people as surely as more dramatized forms of violence do, and in larger numbers. And while you won't see "economically trapped by late-stage capitalism in a food desert" on someone's death certificate, that would be honest.

Fortunately, there's a lot being done in this area that deserves celebration. Here's a handful of examples of how this tool has been more radically employed in the last decade:

The Black Oaks Center for Sustainable Renewable Living

I met Dr. Jifunza Wright Carter at a conference in 2015 where we were both speaking. She told me a number of fascinating stories about the founding of her home project, The Black Oaks Center for Sustainable Renewable Living, located south of Chicago in a traditionally black farming community. Its stated purpose is to assist communities in reducing their carbon footprint and fossil fuel use.

Jifunza is a medical doctor, and one of the many explorations that led to the founding of the project was a recognition that true healing needs both community and direct connection to the land. Her son (at the age of nine) brought her and her husband Fred's attention to resource depletion and climate change, and that set the whole family on the road to integrating a deep understanding of the black community's traditional relationship to the land, and to focusing on using that heritage as a powerful tool to address climate change and community empowerment. They are committed to a strong urban-rural partnership, focused on growing food and healing.

Today their projects include seed banking, permaculture training, an organic food buying club, and an outdoor leadership training that over 500 adults and children have participated in.

Urban Farming in Detroit

[A] wide-ranging transformation is taking place in response to the devastation and disaster of our deindustrialized city. Instead of viewing ourselves as victims, grassroots Detroiters are discovering and embracing the power within us to create ourselves and our world anew. ...Detroiters are carrying on the African American tradition of "making a way out of no way."

—the Feedom Freedom blog[44]

Truly urban farming is both very much like its rural counterpart (after all, the plants need what they need, regardless of where the city limits are drawn)

---

[44] March 8, 2011, "A Whole New Culture by Grace Lee Boggs," feedomfreedom.wordpress .com/2011/03/08/a-whole-new-culture-by-grace-lee-boggs.

and very different. Case in point: the **Keep Growing Detroit**[45] website prominently features a soil sample survey they conducted city-wide and tells their constituents that 19% of the samples indicate lead levels too high to grow food safely. Concentrated human populations have led to concentrated pollution for centuries—thus, things the *Farmers' Almanac* doesn't have to spend much time on, urban farmers everywhere are savvily mindful about, including lead. Keep Growing Detroit provides a range of support services, from education to technical support, from organizing work parties to engaging the City of Detroit around issues such as land security for the gardens.

And they aren't alone: people are growing an increasing amount of food in urban centers, a phenomenon that seems to be a combination of practicality, survival technique, and rebellion in action. The outcomes are multifaceted: raised property values, saved money on groceries for participating families, and $1.5 million in annual income for urban farmers are all reported by Keep Growing Detroit, and *National Geographic* notes that urban farms provide green spaces and reduced food miles for the cities they occupy.

Remember, this is Detroit—the city that most of America seems to have written off as a wasteland of urban failure: that was certainly the main narrative I was raised on, growing up in Michigan in the '70s and '80s. Seen through the lens of urban agriculture, Detroit is not a failure so much as a city whose people have demonstrated a remarkable ability to determine their own needs and creatively meet them, despite governmental neglect and widespread bashing from the rest of the country. And it seems that one of the key factors in this grassroots revitalization is food.

Detroit may well be the Cuba of America: a place that hit economic and resource meltdown (in both cases, based more on politics than natural limits) a half century before most of the rest of the country and thus can be seen as a model for how the rest of us can pull ourselves out of the kind of crisis that is spreading quickly. Detroit is powerful for a number of reasons, including that the state government care often seems to run the gamut from apathetic, to fatally neglectful, to downright hostile: remember, Flint, Michigan, with its well-publicized and still largely undealt-with (as of this writing) lead crisis, is just up the road. That's just one of many stories of a pattern of neglect in Michigan's cities.

So let's take a very quick look at some of the other projects happening in just one US city:

Feedom Freedom (whose blog tagline is "Grow a Garden, Grow a Community") provides a strong cultural and political analysis of urban farming in Detroit, and it echoes some of what I'm exploring in this book around the need for cultural shift, not just eco-technology.

---

[45] detroitagriculture.net seems to be a hub of information about urban farming programs in the city. Thanks to Jacob Corvidae and Tawana Petty for helping me sort through the dizzying array of projects happening in Detroit to find this starting place.

This cultural revolution is very different from the cultural revolution involving the education of mostly illiterate Russian peasants advocated by Lenin after the Bolshevik seizure of state power in 1917. It is also very different from Mao's 1966 cultural revolution which sent millions of educated Chinese youth to work in the countryside and learn from the peasantry. It goes beyond the cultural revolution of the '60s which began to redefine race, gender, generational relations.

Today's cultural revolution, which is emerging from the ground up especially in Detroit, is as awesome as the transition from Hunting and Gathering to Agriculture 11,000 years ago and from Agriculture to Industry a few hundred years ago.

Forty years ago Wayne Curtis was a Black Panther. Now a soft-spoken man with gray dreadlocks, he and his wife Myrtle Thompson are co-founders of Feedom Freedom Growers, a community garden which is revitalizing their east side neighborhood, supplying fresh produce to local restaurants, and energizing and educating schoolkids by giving them opportunities to be of use now by doing work that is real, like growing food.

They are also growing hearts and minds.[46]

In addition to a thought-provoking blog, Feedom Freedom also provides an impressive amount of networking, with an extensive bulletin board of related events happening locally to keep people engaged and informed about meetings, parties, workshops, community clean-ups, and other happenings that concretely affect their lives. While I'm sure there is far more happening in Detroit than any one group can keep track of, an aspiring activist wouldn't go wrong simply using their website as their calendar of events. Feedom Freedom's goals include strengthening the local economy and increasing safety for residents.

The Detroit Black Community Food Security Network (DBCFSN) formed to address food insecurity in Detroit's Black community, and to organize members of that community to play a more active leadership role in the local food security movement. The founders recognized that there were discrepancies between who was leading the food security movement in Detroit (mostly young white activists) and who was being served (mostly the local African American population) and that, however well-intentioned, this was perpetuating unhealthy power dynamics. They decided to build their leadership from within and launched the DBFSN in 2006.

"DBCFSN is creating model urban agricultural projects that seek to build community self-reliance, and to change our consciousness about food."[47] In a fairly holistic approach, DBCFSN has three layers of activities: urban agriculture, policy development, and cooperative buying, and has an active farm, called D-Town Farm, within city limits.

---

[46] feedomfreedom.wordpress.com

[47] Information and this quote come from the group's website: detroitblackfoodsecurity.org.

Finally, the **Oakland Avenue Urban Farm** is a program of North End Christian Community Development Corporation. Their goals are to grow healthy foods, nurture sustainable economies, and provide active cultural environments for local residents. They style themselves the nation's "first Agri-Cultural" center, and the project includes farms on the north end of Detroit, a farm store, and a farmers' market. This project directly addresses the food desert phenomenon in this neighborhood.

All of this adds up to a vibrant, grassroots, culturally appropriate set of responses to the systemic racism of our national food system, and it is using community as a primary organizing principle, both philosophically and tangibly. Similarly vibrant scenes are happening in cities all over the US, including Los Angeles and New York. It seems to me that Feedom Freedom has it right: growing gardens *is* growing community.

Great Idea 2: Meal Sharing

Food is one of the true universals: everyone eats. Most of us have familial and cultural associations with food, and we have developed an incredible range of ways to get our food needs met (both technologically and in terms of the contents of our diets). This makes food rich and interesting territory for sharing, which is pretty handy since, several times a day, most of us need to put some energy into feeding ourselves. So why not share labor and resources, reduce our time spent prepping food, and tap into that richness that emerges almost immediately when we get other people involved with our food scene?[48]

I love this little meal sharing anecdote from EcoVillage at Ithaca's blog:

> Adriane Wolfe is an action-oriented entrepreneur. When she has a good idea, she pursues it with enthusiasm. For her master's degree in energy systems engineering, she researched electricity usage in EcoVillage's first neighborhood. By analyzing neighborhood-wide data as well as individual household usage, she noticed something interesting: on nights when there were community meals in our cohousing neighborhood, overall electricity usage plummeted. What was most surprising is that evening peak energy usage for participating households dropped by a whopping 32%.[49]

This quote gets at one of the underestimated benefits of meal sharing: assuming you aren't driving long distances to meet your food buddies, it saves a lot of energy as well as the accompanying carbon emissions. In addition to having the lights running only in one place, it also takes less fuel to make the food. Cooking one bigger pot of beans for 20 people simply takes less gas or electricity than the same number of people cooking six smaller pots of beans.

---

[48] See *Communites* #167, Summer 2015, "Food and Community," available at www. ic.org/community-bookstore/product/communities-magazine-167-summer-2015-food-and-community.

[49] The post is called *Want to Save Energy? Eat Together*. November 13, 2016, by Liz Walker.

It also saves time overall: one cook spending three hours to make a meal for those 20 people is better than six cooks each spending an hour.

Two other benefits of meal sharing: 1) We are able to get a chunk of our social needs met doing something we'd have to do anyway. Food in America is often a pretty isolating experience. The worst is when we go through a drive-through and then eat in the car on the way somewhere, but a surprisingly large percentage of our meals are eaten alone.[50] 2) When we cook less frequently, we often find ourselves taking more care with the meals we do cook, resulting in more carefully planned and executed meals. In short, it is easier to love cooking when it isn't quite such a daily drudgery. If you meal share even twice a week, that means two nights a week where all you have to do most of the time is show up and you can have a lovingly cooked meal ready for the eating and sharing. Then when it is your turn, you can take the time to offer it to your friends as an act of love.

So here's a simple formula for creating a meal sharing program that embodies ecological values, love, and reduced work load for all participants:

- Find two to six other people or families who want to participate. This is enough people to be able to get at least some labor sharing benefits, but not so many that most people's houses can't accommodate the group. If only one person has a big enough space, then work out an agreement that works for everyone for their place to be the eating hub.

- Choose people who are either within walking or biking distance of each other or on the way to (or from) other places you drive anyway.

- Make some simple agreements about what things can be served (and have to be served) in order for the meals to work well for the members. This may mean, for example, always needing to include a vegetarian protein option, and avoiding things people are allergic to.

- Rotate cooking. If not everyone loves to cook, they can be on clean-up duty. If not everyone feels confident in cooking for a group, offer to have buddies at the start until people gain the confidence to be able to cook. If you have a big enough pool of cooks, you can actually cook in pairs all the time if you like.

- Make leftovers agreements and bring your own containers from home.

- Consider having collective equipment that can go to whoever is cooking next. A big crock pot, a haybox,[51] large pots and pans, and an electric coffee urn are all examples of things a single person or family might

---

[50] A study by the Hartman Group, reported on NPR, indicates that 46% of "adult eating occasions" are done solo, including about one quarter of our dinners.

[51] A haybox is simply an insulated box that you can use to finish a dish without using a lot of energy. You bring your food (grains, soups, or beans) up to a full boil for five to 15 minutes (depending on the item) and then take it off the heat and put it into the box. The food then passively finishes cooking, and never burns. The simplest haybox is a cooler with an old towel or blanket

not own, but are very useful when cooking for bigger groups.

- Finally, consider how you can use your meal sharing to organize for deeper change: watch a political movie together once a month and talk; use this as a first step in starting a community; encourage people to bring petitions or announcements of actions happening in the area; or simply invite deeper conversation than is normal for our culture, thereby becoming a part of each other's real support networks. It's best to not make every meal political, but there's no sense wasting a perfectly good platform to take things deeper.

Variations on the standard theme of this meal sharing system I describe above include hosting an underground restaurant (if one of your friends loves cooking for big groups a lot, this could be a good alternative: they cook, and everyone else pays for the ingredients and leaves tips for the cook, leaving the cook to eat for free) or doing a cooking swap where each person cooks a meal that can be easily frozen for everyone else and you meet once a week to trade meals you've prepared for each other. This gets less of your social needs met, but has many of the other advantages.

Great Idea 3: Car Sharing

Car sharing programs are one of those things that were pioneered in intentional communities (income sharing communities in particular—it's pretty much a no-brainer to share cars when you are sharing money) and have since gained some real traction in the wider culture. Zipcar, Relay Rides, and Car to Go are all prominent programs that seem to have functional structures. With 625,000 members of Zipcar alone in 2011, these programs are serving a large number of urban residents.

A Transportation Research Board/National Academy of Sciences study finds each shared car takes about 15 private cars off the road. And that is impacting the industry: Alix Partners[52] has estimated that a half million cars have not been purchased in the US because of these programs. That's a lot of resources not consumed. Here are a few other statistics about one program, Zipcar:

- Each car share member reduces their personal CO_2 emissions by between 1,100 and 1,600 pounds per year.[53] Collectively, the estimated CO_2 reduction from Zipcar members is between 685 million and 1 billion pounds, for the year ending 2011.

---

inside it for extra insulation, which is wrapped around the pot. It's my favorite simple energy saving technology. For more information, see "The Haybox Cooker: Why Every Community Needs One" in *Communities* #115 and in *Best of Communities* volume 10, both available at ic.org.

[52] A consulting and business advisory firm that was highlighted in a Feb. 14, 2004 CNBC article online about car sharing.

[53] Susan Shaheen and Elliot Martin, *Greenhouse Gas Emission Impacts of Car Sharing in North America* (San Jose State University, 2010).

- Zipcar members report saving an average of $600 per month compared to owning a car.[54]

- Car sharing seems to encourage "good" behavior ecologically in other ways: members report a 46% increase in public transit trips, a 10% increase in bicycling trips, and a 26% increase in walking trips.[55]

- And for a statistic that might be of particular interest to city planners, North American car sharing programs average 49 members to every vehicle, reducing the overall number of cars on the road and decreasing the need for more parking spots.[56]

In addition to savings of money, carbon emissions, parking spaces, and time spent maintaining a personal car, many car share programs also offer flexibility: you can drive a small hybrid one day, a large passenger van the next, and access a pickup truck when needed through some of these programs.

Car share programs are available in many major cities. A partial list includes: Portland (Oregon), the San Francisco Bay Area, New York, Boston, Denver, Houston, Philadelphia, Seattle, and Chicago, as well as a number of smaller cities. Transition US provides a basic information sheet for people interested in starting a formal program in their area, including pointing to more nuts and bolts resources for getting started.

The Casual Car Share

Car shares can also be organized at a very casual level. During the last year that I lived in Albuquerque, New Mexico before moving back to Dancing Rabbit in 2008, I owned a car that had multiple other users who weren't part of my household.

One friend needed to use a car once or twice a week for quick errands. Another was splitting her time between California and Albuquerque and needed a car just for a weekend or two each month (which happened to be when I didn't use mine much at all). The three of us worked out a simple arrangement: they'd pay me $8/day each day they used it,[57] leave the tank more full than they got it, and if they went over a certain number of miles in a day, they'd pay an extra fee. Finally, if they got into an accident, they'd be responsible for whatever costs were incurred because of that.

For them, this was far less expensive than owning their own car only for it to sit there most of the time. For me, it felt a lot better to have more people using

---

[54] Adam Millard-Ball, Gail Murray, Jessica ter Schure, Christine Fox, and Jon Burkhardt, "Car-Sharing: Where and How It Succeeds." In *Transit Cooperative Research Program*, Report 108; Transportation Research Board, 2005.

[55] Ibid.

[56] Frost and Sullivan,"Strategic Analysis of Carsharing Market in North America." January 2010.

[57] We calculated the $8/day fee based on adding up what I generally spent to have the car on a monthly basis (insurance, maintenance costs, and my car payment) and divided by three, since there were three of us adults using the car regularly.

what I knew was a valuable asset instead of its sitting idle regularly, and I felt good about two other people not needing to buy a car—I was doing my own little anti-new-manufacture campaign. And a little extra money was nice, too.

Obviously, these were high-trust relationships: a casual set-up like that won't work otherwise. Still, if you have that kind of trust, you could—pardon the pun—get a lot of mileage out of this relatively simple idea, reducing all of your ecological impact and costs. Casual car sharing with people with compatible needs and use patterns in your neighborhood is a great way to start car sharing. It could also be a simple and organic way to start the process of creating a more formal car share.

Great Idea 4: Alternative Currencies: Within Intentional Communities and Beyond

I wrote about Dancing Rabbit's local currency earlier. This is a tool that is particularly potent in community, but actually has a lot of promise outside of that realm.

To help me understand how these currencies and exchange systems work, I called on Chong Kee Tan.[58] Chong Kee is one of the most remarkable activists I know. He went from taking on a repressive government in his homeland of Singapore over freedom of press issues to creating one of the more interesting local currencies in the US, the catchily named Bay Bucks.

For Chong Kee, the crash of 2008 was a big wake-up call. He says that he was disturbed to realize that "we have a system that destroys our environment, impoverishes future generations for the benefit of a very tiny minority." His point about impoverishing future generations is well taken: Millennials are the first generation that is decidedly worse off financially than their parents, according to both the UK-based think tank Resolution Foundation and the Pew Research Foundation here in the US.

In the process of considering what happened, he realized that how we do money was currently incredibly problematic; more importantly, he realized that changing that system had the potential to be a powerful tool for social change. It's a lot about power, and moving away from exchange that leaches money out of projects and local communities and into Wall Street. The blanket term that Chong Kee uses for alternative monetary systems that he studies is "mutual credit" systems. He explained it to me this way:

> Mutual credit is a monetary system that allows users to issue or create money, rather than giving banks the monopoly of money issuance. Money as a means of exchange is just a way to track value exchanges between people. To have integrity, monetary systems must be accountable, mean-

---

[58] I was already familiar with Chong Kee's work through our overlapping activism with two organizations: The Center for Sustainable and Cooperative Culture (Dancing Rabbit's nonprofit) and Commonomics USA (an economic and ecological justice organization). I also interviewed him on Dec. 29, 2016.

ing, no entity can unilaterally increase or decrease the money supply to extract wealth. The problem with governments printing money is that they are often tempted to print more and more to pay for government spending, which leads to runaway inflation. Giving the power to issue money to private banks who create money when a consumer wants to borrow seemed like a good solution.

Unfortunately, they have discovered how to game this system and used unethical tactics such as predatory lending, mortgage backed security, and credit default swap that eventually crashed the global economy. Community MC currency solves this problem by democratizing the issuance of money, so that the money supply corresponds to real demand. And there are no financial instruments like credit default swap, making it impossible to play destructive financial games.

Two underlying messages in this really stand out for me. The first is simply that we don't have to do finance the way we do it right now: we have options, and a number of them are far better for the 99%. The second is that Chong Kee has laid out a basic framework, within which a lot of different creative systems could be developed, so long as they are, as he says, "accountable and consensual." The big bank-centered system we have right now is neither of those.

So let's look at some examples of where else the idea of a localized and democratized exchange are happening to good effect:

The Credito at Damanhur in Italy

What would happen if a local community insisted that their system of exchange be congruent with the values they had founded that community on? One ecovillage in Italy decided to pursue this idea, and they created their own local currency, exchangeable one-for-one with the euro.

From the Damanhur website:

> The *Credito* is Damanhur's complementary currency system. The community's objective in creating this coinage was to develop a new form of economy based on the ethical values of cooperation and solidarity. The *Credito* is a return to the use of money in its original meaning: as a means to facilitate exchange, based on an agreement between those involved. The word *"credito"* (credit) reminds us that money is a tool through which we grant trust. This currency system raises the concept of money to a more noble status. It is not considered a goal in and of itself, but rather a functional tool for exchange between people who share ideals and values.[59]

Creditos are used for all internal exchange within Damanhur. Unlike Dancing Rabbit's system, which is handled via an online exchange program, creditos are actually minted. Interestingly enough, the credito is legit enough

---

[59] www.damanhur.org/en/live-community/economy-and-work.

that you can find them on the international currency exchange website NGC coin, tradable among specialty coin traders like any other "real" currency.

Time Banking in Los Angeles...and the World

In 13 neighborhoods of Los Angeles, over 1,000 people (including members of the Los Angeles Ecovillage) participate in the Arroyo S.E.C.O. Network of Time Banks. In this system, services are traded among members hour for hour in what they call a "pay it forward system": someone provides a service for another person in the network and then has an hour of credit they can trade in for receiving a service from another person. You do not need to trade hour for hour with the same person, and there are also goods that can be exchanged using credits, both of which allow for a good deal of flexibility in the system.

The Time Bank also sponsors community events (including Tai Chi and Spanish classes and a gardening club), providing more opportunity for members to meet and build trust and connection.

One of the stated purposes of the Time Bank is to break down the separation between people with needs and people who provide for needs. The idea is to acknowledge that we are all in both categories in different ways, and to personalize that.

The Arroyo S.E.C.O. Time Bank is part of an international network of time banks called hOurworld that lists 651 communities doing time banking around the world. They provide resources for groups to get started, including software, and have as one purpose to "circumvent our scarcity based cash economy."

Bay Bucks, San Francisco

Getting an alternative currency or exchange network off the ground isn't easy. A number of attempts have been made in the US that eventually folded. One of the keys to a system's success is people being able to acquire some basic need, such as food or clothing. If the only services are, say, dentistry and cakes, then there isn't going to be much vibrancy to your system (no matter how enthusiastic the dentist and good the cakes).

So Bay Bucks started with a unique approach: it has initially been an exchange between businesses (and their employees) who are part of a trade exchange. This has helped keep the emphasis on building the local economy through empowering businesses, and has enrolled the business community in peer-to-peer recruiting and conversations about local economy issues. Since one of the very necessary aspects of getting this off the ground, according to Chong Kee, is education about economics, having business owners actively talking to each other has built in an educational element that might have been missed had they gone directly to individuals. That said, with about $100K of business to business exchanges, Bay Bucks is feeling robust enough that they will soon be opening it up to individual members.

The primary talking points on the Bay Bucks website are localism and anti-exploitation. They name these four things as reasons to get involved:

- You are supporting your local businesses.

- You are ensuring that 100% of the money you spend will stay in the local community.

- You are using a currency that does not exploit people or the planet.

- You are participating in a larger movement to help build a new, equitable economic paradigm.[60]

I like this list in part because in a very short space you can see all four dimensions of sustainability in action: a paradigm change (worldview), community and non-exploitation of people (social), non-exploitation of the earth and buying more locally (ecological), and of course the whole thing is leveraged through an economic choice.

This kind of very holistic system is what is needed to move the whole culture (and not just intentional communities) toward real sustainability. Bay Bucks is a great example of what intelligent, diligent, creative action looks like.

---

[60] www.baybucks.com.

Chapter 3: Surviving It

Let me be clear about where I stand on the topic of climate disruption in general: I believe we have already crossed lines that can't be uncrossed, that climate disruption is the new normal, and that we have done this to ourselves.

Millions of people are already experiencing climate apocalypse: ask refugees from Syria whose lives have become a tangled mess of heavy-handed politics, environmental destruction, and blatant racism. The endless videos of bleeding, shell-shocked Syrian children on Facebook, crying for their dead or missing parents, bring home in the most painful way the message that we have already gone past the point of no return.[61]

Ask the indigenous water protectors at Standing Rock and the people at hundreds of other indigenous-led protest sites around the world: they and their ancestors have been living with the realities of a mainstream populace disconnected from both their fellow humans and the soul-restoring wilds for generations. They have seen and felt this moment coming for a long time.

Ask the millions of people who have already lost their homes to flood and sea level rise in the Maldive Islands, in Louisiana, and in other low-lying places; or to wildfires in the western US and Canada; or to fracking-caused earthquakes in Oklahoma...and who have then found little sympathy or support from their own governments and other governments whose nations have significant responsibility for climate change.

Or just pay attention to the news.

I did some rough, back-of-the envelope calculations during one particular week in the summer of 2016. As I saw images of 30,000 homes under water in Louisiana and simultaneous mass evacuations because of fires in California, it occurred to me that there were a LOT of Americans displaced right

---

[61] Many people are unaware that the current Syrian refugee crisis has a strong tie-in to climate change. The trouble in Syria began with a major drought. Families lost their farms, and the government ignored them when they asked for help. So, many people began relocating to the cities and sending money home from city jobs. Further requests for help were similarly ignored, and anger started to rise. The rebellion and subsequent crackdown began with the disruption of age-old weather patterns. Thus, all of these Syrian refugees can be legitimately labeled climate refugees. And that does not bode well for our collective future at all. To learn more, check out a *Scientific American* article from Dec. 17, 2015 by John Wendle: "The Ominous Story of Syria's Climate Refugees."

at that moment because of climate disruption. And sure enough, after cross-checking the numbers estimates among several articles in each case and taking a middle-of-the-road number, the total was shocking: for a period of about 48 hours, approximately *one in a thousand* Americans were experiencing climate change-related displacement. And that was just new displacements: I didn't count all the people who have never gotten back in their homes from Hurricanes Katrina and Sandy, and other long-term displacements.

It is simply a matter of time before this crisis circles close enough to touch those who haven't already felt its sting. And yet, we keep barreling further down the road to destruction. That is, to put it mildly, insane.

We need to figure some things out about how to survive in this new reality, and we need to do it quickly.

The Apocalypse Cometh

Linguists tell us that the word "apocalypse" may not mean what most of us think it means. The word comes from Greek, and it means something close to "uncovering," "revealing," or "a moment of discovery." We are in a time when we are stripping away illusions of all sorts—political, relational, economic, and ecological.

When we discard the systems and beliefs that got us here, we are left with the fundamental building blocks of something new: our passion, creativity, and labor. Our ability to hold the planet as sacred, and hold each other accountable. Our skills, and whatever amount of evolution we've come to in our consciousness.

These things are real, and yet they often get buried so deeply—by profit motive, a host of oppressive -isms, and a competitive, independent drive that has come to be confused with "success"—that our everyday experience of them is clouded, and they are inaccessible as tools for our lives. I believe that if anything is being "revealed" right now, it is these things. Welcome to the apocalypse: zombie gear (apparently) not needed.

Instead, stripped down by the economic and ecological realities of our time, we are left with our selves and each other. And that's actually a pretty good place to start.

Economics: Getting Our Needs Met

The big fear most people seem to have when we start talking about changing our ecological practices is a very primal fear around not being able to get our needs met. And that's huge. Economic insecurity is terrifying for most people, perhaps especially for people who have never really experienced it in any long-term way. Any talk about change, or resilience, or new ways of living has to effectively address how we get our needs met, or it is a non-starter.

Economics in the US is generally thought of as the study and mechanics of money. It is taught in schools as the science of dollars, how dollars relate to goods and services, and markets using dollars. I believe this is far too narrow of a perception of what economics is about. Economics in my mind is the science of how we get our needs met.

What follows is a five-part radical reorienting of how we think about economics and what it means to each of us. As you are reading, consider how all communities can foster a healthier way of being in terms of how we get our needs met.

There are five basic categories for how we get our needs met. I'm using "things" here as shorthand to mean both goods and services.

1. Things we currently define as needs that can be eliminated or significantly reduced.

2. Things that can be shared, reducing the individual burden.

3. Things that can be done for oneself (DIY, or do it yourself).

4. Things that can be bartered or traded for.

5. Things that require money to acquire or get access to.

Most Americans (at least Americans who are not living in poverty) have all or nearly all of their needs met in the last category, meaning that we use money almost exclusively as our medium of exchange and our tool for getting our needs met. That category is the furthest removed from our real human relationships, and the category that puts you into the most direct contact with the banking industry's practices and exploitation.

This is an important piece: banks, as we currently operate them, are fundamentally extractive entities. From the Public Banking Institute's website:

> In the case of nearly every state and town government, it is standard practice to send millions upon millions of dollars a year to banks and investors to pay the interest on bonds that have been issued for state infrastructure. If you add up the money the towns collectively send to banks and investors for the same purposes, it is a lot of money. In the case of California, its long awaited new Bay Bridge span was recently completed at a cost of $6.4 billion—over 400% over its initial projection. What most Californians don't realize is that the total cost of the bridge will eclipse $13 billion when interest payments are considered over their life. 50% of costs going toward interest payments…is not an aberration—it is pretty much a standard calculation.[62]

---

[62] www.publicbankinginstitute.org/faq. These statements are based largely on the work of Ellen Brown, author of *The Public Bank Solution*. The way this works is that loan interest is accumulated through the various stages of business relationships. For example, getting a school built requires loans which come with a certain amount of interest. They are built by businesses who may have their own loans to keep their doors open, buy materials up front, etc., and that interest raises their prices…and the businesses they subcontract with have the same layers of interest built into their business plans. And if anyone in this chain is renting business space, those owners may well have a mortgage they are paying off (more interest!), the costs of which

The same is true of any entity (including businesses and individuals) whose needs get met in any way that involves interest payments. So if we want to not just be feeding Wall Street, it's best to get our needs met in the earlier stages of this model.

Getting our needs met in those other ways requires a combination of self-awareness, physical work, and social relationship skills. Not everyone has abilities in all of those areas, but nearly everyone is capable of at least one of those categories. Every time someone cooks a meal at home instead of going to McDonalds, carpools or rides a bike to work, helps a neighbor move so they don't have to hire help to do it, decides to not buy the newest gadget, shops at a thrift store, brews their own beer, or loans a friend $200 interest-free until payday, they are making economic decisions to meet a need in a way that rebels against the money-based paradigm.

Let's look more closely at all five categories.

1. Things we currently define as needs that can be eliminated or significantly reduced.

   This is about consuming less, and rethinking what we mean by "needs." It is a consciousness shift that looks toward things like relationships and voluntary simplicity to create a better quality of life. There are yuppie versions of this, à la Sarah Susankas "Not So Big..." books that emphasize quality over quantity, but are still very much focused on material wealth. Then there are more radical versions of this like Lauren Singer, the young woman who creates a quart's worth of trash in a year, Duane Elgin's *Voluntary Simplicity*, and the Tiny House movement.

   It is about fundamentally questioning what things like happiness and security are, and then buying less. Buy Nothing Day hints at this and does a good job of drawing attention to excessive consumerism, but it is a one-day event in the sea of mass consumerism.

   Reducing what we think of as needs is the first step to having an easier time meeting them for your average American. Poor people are generally experts at this already, simply because they can't afford excess, and I want to emphasize that voluntary simplicity and poverty are very different things from systemically enforced poverty. Poor countries just consume less than wealthier ones, and many ecological-footprint people say you can get a ballpark read on what someone's ecological footprint is simply by knowing how much money they spent in the last year.

   Remember that Dancing Rabbit consumes only 14% of the average American's electricity: that's some seriously reduced need, and a lot of

---

they pass on to their renters. Add it all up, and the main financial beneficiaries are on Wall Street, not in the communities of the families whose kids go to that school; and taxpayers foot the bill.

that comes at the household decision level: not just turning off lights but also building homes with abundant natural light; not just drying clothes on the line, but washing them only when they are actually dirty, not simply when they have touched your body for a few hours. Being conscientious goes a long way to seriously reducing what we think of as needs.

2. Things that can be shared, reducing the individual burden.

This is where the community in its myriad forms comes in. I'm excited about all forms of institutional and community-organized sharing, including car share programs, tool libraries, intentional communities, community gardens, local currencies, and time banks, as well as long-standing examples of this like public libraries and urban green spaces. Not only do we need a lot less than we think we do, we also don't need nearly as much of it to be held as private property.

Sharing also develops our ability to build relationships that are often invaluable when a crisis happens. For instance, I basically lost three years of my life to chronic lyme disease, and what got me through that without ending up completely destitute was the community bonds and systems I had put in place by being part of Dancing Rabbit. Other people lean on their church communities when this happens—there are lots of ways to create it, but the point of my example is that community *is* health coverage in some significant ways.

There are also community-level examples of very radical economic models, and that includes income sharing. Living in one of those communities for two and a half years really changed my relationship and thinking on what "productive work" is. What I learned more than anything else is that the world has no lack of productive work to do—but it does have a lack of *jobs*. That is likely to continue to be more and more true as automation continues to eliminate jobs. Thus it seems timely to be questioning the basic assumption that we get our needs met through money, and we get our money through jobs.

This second category is also where socialization comes in. It would seem crazy to people if everyone had to build their own section of road in front of their houses—at this point, nearly everyone has accepted in the US that some things are obviously better done on a large collective scale. The EPA serves a critical role in keeping air and water clean… and yet because privatization and business rights are also a big part of people's thinking (and air quality less easy to discern for most people than potholes) we are not collectively as sold on this being obviously to the good.

I place a strong value in the government **getting out of the way of local organizing efforts** (repealing laws that limit the number of unrelated adults who can cohabitate, for instance) **while playing a more**

active role in supporting community-based sharing and responsibility, including large-scale infrastructure—state or federal level—for those systems that could be best socialized on that scale (the aforementioned roads, and healthcare, for instance). This isn't about small versus large government, it is about *different* government: what if the government's job were to help us share more effectively, instead of protecting private property and ecologically destructive business rights? (See Chapter 6 for more on that.)

Another point in favor of sharing is that we can take advantage of economies of scale. Buying food in bulk is just the beginning. In the US, there are about four cars for every five people (including children, who surely aren't driving them)...closing in on a 1:1 ratio. And yet how much actual time do we spend in our cars? Most of the time, any given car is just sitting there. Dancing Rabbit has a car to human ratio of about 4:60...that's one vehicle for every 15 people. That's a lot fewer cars to maintain, finance, and protect from the elements. And even at Dancing Rabbit, there are days when all of the cars just sit there.

You can also scale labor in community. One person cooking a meal for 10 people (or 30 or 100) takes less time, creative juice, and fuel than the more normal four people cooking for 10, 12 people cooking for 30, or 30-some people cooking for 100. That frees up tremendous time and energy overall, while saving on fossil fuels (or whatever fuel you might be using to cook with). Two people taking care of 10 kids for an afternoon is a lot more efficient than each set of parents having to dedicate half their available workforce to that activity.

Sharing is simple math, but the impact on real people is huge.

3. Things that can be done for oneself (a.k.a. DIY).

Doing-It-Yourself (DIY) is still powerful. That garden in the backyard that produces half a family's produce for the summer; the basic skills to do everything from clean your own chimney to fix meals at home to troubleshoot plumbing problems before you need to spend $50 an hour for someone else to come deal with your sink; the attitude that I'm going to ride my bike as much as possible to avoid paying for gas and keep my body healthier; the ability to make and competently use basic medicines at home; the creativity to make a chunk of your own fun instead of bar-hopping and driving across town to a movie; sewing your own clothes and making your own wine...all of these are examples of DIY, and it can save a ton of money.[63]

DIY is direct needs-fulfillment; jobs are not.

---

[63] Note that there is an obvious trade-off here between time and money. Many poor people are poor in both time and money, and it takes time to build up a lot of DIY skills. Thus, it is important when we start advocating for people doing more DIY to be sensitive to the class implications of that advocacy.

Consider how jobs work for most of us: we work at a job (driving there and burning fossil fuels that cost money) to get money and then go to the store (burning more fossil fuels which cost more money) to buy something that is relatively impersonal. Add on top of the aforementioned costs of having a job things like wardrobe requirements, the challenges of feeding yourself well and cheaply on the go, and the need for childcare while at work, and you start to see that jobs are actually a weirdly expensive way to get your needs met.

Instead DIY cuts out those middle steps and you use your hours in direct engagement with your need. This can do a lot of things for you: build confidence, avoid the rat race, and also avoid the extra expenditure of money in the form of interest that ultimately ends up in the hands of banksters and which may keep you feeling stuck in that job you may not like very much.

I think of the difference between DIY and the job-money-consume paradigms as similar to having a home that is passive-solar heated versus one heated using fossil fuels (that also came from the sun but with many steps between sun and the heat that comes out of your ducts). Or like the problems with line loss in huge electricity grids—every step loses a little bit of energy and is less efficient, has a lot of unintended consequences, requires little actual understanding or direct engagement about where heat comes from (and therefore dumbs us all down a bit), and ultimately doesn't yield anything that is more satisfying or useful.

There's a disconnect that disturbs me as well—we are not living life anymore so much as skimming over the top of it, wondering why we feel numb and disconnected. There's a spiritual "line loss" as well as a physical one.

DIY reminds us that we do not need dollars to survive; we need to get our needs met to survive.

If you can meet a bunch of your own needs without requiring a job to acquire the medium of exchange to get those needs met, you gain freedom from a lot of systems that are built on oppression of various sorts. Collectively, we also gain resilience when we can meet our needs in ways that are more timeless and not so culturally and socially-specific. If you believe (as I do) that systems change or collapse is coming down the pipeline to North America, then getting a jump on learning these skills is what resilience is all about.

4. Things that can be bartered or traded for.

This could be in hours banks or other barter networks that are formalized, or casual labor exchange between neighbors. Barter systems tend to strengthen social relationships, which also provide a greater safety net for many of us. Just about anything in the form of services or products an individual or small group produces can be a candidate for barter, and this can be at the level of tomatoes for eggs, legal services for massage, or help on this Saturday for help next Saturday.

Most interesting from an educational standpoint is actually to mix up those kinds of categories. How many eggs are worth an hour of legal services? Is an hour-long massage the same to you as an hour of raking leaves in someone's yard? Is it different with someone you know than someone you just met? You can get a very clear read on how you value both what you have to offer and what others have to offer by doing conscious barter. I'm recommending in Chapter 5 that we do personal work around class and classism, and self-awareness during a barter exchange is a very interesting experiment to start with.

Barter also opens the door for conflict in some interesting ways. Do you feel devalued by the conversations that happen? Are you uncomfortable talking about the "worth" of what you offer, and is it hard for you to separate that from your inherent worth as a person? The monetary system often protects us from having to get into these very sticky conversations, and therefore from conflicts (either internal or external) that might arise as we become more aware of the "hard feelings" a lot of us carry around money and/or questions of worth.

Barter exposes those fault lines that our economic system has created in our social relationships. It is worth doing for that alone.

5. Things that require money to acquire or get access to.

From one radical perspective, every time you have to spend an actual dollar on something, that represents a failure: in consciousness, creativity, culture, social relationships, and skills. I personally find that perspective to lack empathy with people who are caught in a system larger than their individual control; I don't think laying the failure label on people is very helpful.

However, I do think we can turn our standard worldview about money on its head: what if we thought of **money as the means of last resort** for fulfilling our needs, rather than the default? Would we push ourselves to be a hell of a lot more creative, to develop more community, and to question a lot of basic assumptions about how our material world works? I think the answer is yes.

Still, the current reality is that most of us have to interact with that wider world and the money paradigm. This is why analyzing the means of financing, banking, and other basic financial structures we are currently locked into is very valuable, and the work of activists. I'll be talking in more depth about financial reform in Chapter 6, including about such ideas as local currencies, public and postal banking, and universal basic income.

The Case for Deeper Communalism

This is a book about climate disruption and community. Looking at structures that foster solid decisions to reduce our ecological and carbon footprints is thus an imperative I have set for myself.

I've been part of the communities movement at this point for over two decades. During that time I have lived in seven different communities, and am in the process of starting the eighth one I hope to live in in a couple years. Those groups were all over the map in terms of structure, proximity to urban centers, spiritual or secular orientations, and how they made decisions. I'm grateful for that range of experiences, and I think they put me in a position of being able to see the pluses, minuses, and implications of each choice pretty clearly.

My first experience with income sharing was a profoundly mixed bag. I loved many things about it: the ease of the system, the sense of security, the feeling of being really at choice with how I spent my time on any given day, and the palpably different gender relationships that resulted from flattening out the money relationships.

But I chafed, too. There wasn't enough opportunity for the kind of professional development I wanted to do, it felt rigid and excessively structured (which is common among larger communities of all sorts, not only income sharing groups), and my partner and I simply couldn't manage our college debts with the small monthly stipend we had to work with. In the end, the drawbacks came to outweigh the good stuff (or maybe I got so acclimated to the good things, I stopped understanding just how powerful they were—for certain, at the age of 28, security wasn't that high on my priority list).

Years later, after being kind of ho-hum about income sharing, I've come back around to being a big enough fan[64] that the group I am helping start in Wyoming will share income.

Here's what shifted:

- As I studied climate change more, I found myself in economic justice circles, and recognized that income sharing can be a kind of secret weapon in overcoming the American worldview of hyper-individualism, including our tendency to hoard resources for individual use.

- One way to speed along the cultural transition I will describe in Chapter 5 is to income share: it drops you solidly into the territory of cooperation instead of competition, into thinking in terms of a healthy "we" instead of an independent "I." My first husband was a former yoga

---

[64] It is important for me to emphasize that what I'm saying here is my view and not necessarily the view of my publisher, the Fellowship for Intentional Community. FIC works with communities of all kinds, and does not actively promote one form over another. While we do promote sustainability as an organization, and therefore will point to income sharing as one good tool for that (using similar thinking to mine above), FIC does not advocate for one form over the other.

monk, and he was fond of quoting one of his Indian teachers as regularly saying, "The problem with Americans is that you think you have to do it all on your own." Income sharing is an effective antidote to that problem.

- Income sharing makes a ton of ecologically responsible decisions into practical no-brainers. Of course we will share cars. Of course we will buy food collectively and therefore in bulk. Of course we will emphasize community space and de-emphasize big, personal spaces. All of those lead to better carbon emissions stats, and those decisions are much less time-consuming to make when collective finances are in play.[65]

- I've also come to see economic justice as a critically important piece of creating the world I want, on its own merits, even if the climate weren't collapsing around us. If a whole group of people commits to living at a roughly similar standard of living, regardless of who is bringing in the money, that's a group that is embodying economic justice.

- Generally speaking, income sharing vastly increases people's options for how they spend their time. Because lots of sharing means less overall money needs to be generated, it opens the door for people focusing more on what they want to focus on. Want to farm? Great! That reduces our collective money needs and is healthier for us, too. Want to take care of kids? Wonderful—that frees up the people who want to cook, or be a lawyer, or teach classes to do their thing and make their contributions, while having their kids cared for by people they trust. Want to cook a lot? Gosh, that's perfect because it needs to happen every day and if you do it a few nights a week that frees up a lot of other people's time to do other stuff. Want to work an intense and stimulating job 50 hours a week and make a bunch of money? Awesome, we need that, too. A little bit of all of the above? Sure, that works!

- Income sharing leads to greater economic resilience for everyone participating. This is simple: if you have one person earning money in a family, or even two, and one of those people loses their job, that's generally disastrous for that economic unit. If you have 15 people in a group doing some kind of money-earning activity, the loss of one job has a much smaller impact. It still might be problematic, but it is unlikely to trigger an immediate financial crisis, and there are a lot more people's skills and energy to draw on to solve that problem.[66]

---

[65] That ease of decision-making is no minor benefit: non-income sharing groups that I've been part of and consulted with have spent many hours agonizing over some decisions that income sharing groups make nearly effortlessly. And that saves countless hours.

[66] That said, some communities as a whole put a lot of their eggs in one industry's basket, and this advantage is blunted in that case. I know groups whose primary income relied on one

- The most common form of secular income sharing has a labor requirement for all members where an hour of income producing work counts the same as an hour of non-income producing work. Valuing all labor equally means that work traditionally unvalued at all (mainly this is domestic tasks that a higher percentage of women still do than men) suddenly is infused with greater dignity and respect. This pulls the lynch pin out of one aspect of systematic sexism, and means that women and men are treated as equals—and by "treated" I don't mean being nicer to women: I mean having an economic system that says in every hour of work done that they are truly equally valued.

- Related to the last two points, standard gender roles also have a tendency to break down when each person has more choice. Turns out a lot of men love doing childcare, organizing space, and cooking. Once the pressure to be "the primary breadwinner" is removed, a surprising percentage of men gravitate toward what has generally been uncompensated domestic labor, a.k.a. "women's work" in the old paradigm. And it also turns out that a lot of women are incredibly competent and interested in work that pays well, and given a real choice, many would rather bring in money than be at home doing that traditional domestic work. And the best news of all is that it isn't an either/or. Many income sharing groups create systems that allow people to do multiple things part-time, which is also a significant freeing thing for most people. And the gender relationships that come out of these systems are palpably different.

That last piece is especially interesting to a lot of people. Income sharing lets you put together the human puzzle in a more humane and consensual way. And consent is important: many people feel they are in a very non-consensual and oppression-based relationship with capitalism right now: they must work jobs they hate to barely get by. It's abusive on a very fundamental level, and that abuse occupies 40–60 hours a week of many people's time, without actually remedying the economic insecurity we are told it will remedy.

No wonder so many of us are walking around with the symptoms of low-level trauma.

As we are starting to look more and more deeply at issues of consent, privilege, and oppression in our culture, classism and economic abuse are going to become bigger parts of that conversation. That is going to cause a lot of us to look twice at the relationships we are in—both interpersonally and with the system we find ourselves in. Income sharing is one way to use that bubble of social experimentation I talked about in the introduction to start weaving a new set of these relationships now.

---

significant account, and when that was lost, the whole community was in crisis. So smart financial planning and economic diversification is still needed in income sharing groups.

In an income sharing group, so long as enough money is coming in and enough meals are getting cooked, etc., people can be much more at choice about how they spend their time. They also have the opportunity to move into a deeper place of integrity with themselves and the planet. How we get our needs met is a core part of how we build self-esteem, as well as how we express our deepest values.

Let's look closely at a community that does income sharing and how this results in ecological gains.

Case Study 2: Twin Oaks Community

Twin Oaks is an income sharing community in Louisa, VA of around 100 residents. Twin Oaks was founded in 1967, and gets high marks for self-sufficiency, including growing an estimated 50% of their own food. The community's goals include "to sustain and expand a community which values cooperation; which is not sexist or racist; which treats people in a caring and fair manner; and which provides for the basic needs of our members...to be a model social system...[that includes] human-scale solutions to problems of land use, food production, energy conservation, and appropriate use of technology."

Twin Oaks is a strongly communal group. They eat all of their meals communally, either in the main dining hall or one of the smaller kitchens scattered throughout the community. No one has a private residence, but rather a room in a dorm with 10–20 people living in it. Solar panels adorn several buildings. They share a fleet of carefully maintained cars, too—about 20 of them for their 100 adults.

The property is heavily wooded, and people's "commute" to work is a walk along a winding forest path, or a short trip in one of the electric golf carts. And they are a full life-cycle community, even having built a hospice facility so that people can remain in a familiar and supportive environment in their final days. For many years, the community has had a hammock-making business, and you can see it in nooks and crannies all over the property—a hammock strung in a courtyard, hammock chairs hanging from the branches of a number of the mature trees on the property—making for mini retreat spaces and social environments. All in all, it is a remarkably pleasant place to live.

The community is similar to Dancing Rabbit in some important ways, including being rural in a middling conservative state, having democratic governance, and utilizing car sharing and common spaces heavily. It differs, though, in a number of key ways too. I'll name two of them here that are most relevant to this book. Twin Oaks did not set out to be an ecovillage, but rather a Walden II community,[67] which means it was intended to be a social

---

[67] *Walden II* is a utopian novel, published in 1948 by B. F. Skinner, a behavioral psychologist. Twin Oaks has evolved significantly over the years and no longer identifies as a behaviorist

experiment more than an ecological one. And the economic structure of the community is also different: Twin Oaks is a commune—they income share.

So how does a community with a similar internal culture and external political environment to Dancing Rabbit, but with *less* original intentionality around sustainability and *more* communal structures compare in terms of the ecological outcomes? The answer is: very well.

Twin Oaks members use no more than 32% of the water of the average American. I say "no more than" because I do not have an easy way to separate business activities happening at Twin Oaks (and in the case of their tofu factory, I suspect that water consumption is a noticeable % of this overall community water usage) and yet national statistics hold the categories of domestic, agricultural, and business uses separately. Twin Oaks is a little too integrated to make for simple comparisons with water. So I derived that number by comparing all of the domestic use and one half of the agricultural use of an average American to Twin Oaks' total usage of water, for domestic, agricultural, and business activities.[68]

The other stats made it a little easier to feel that I was comparing apples to apples. Compared with the average American's domestic consumption, Twin Oaks members:

- use 24% of the electricity
- use 17% of the propane and
- drive 17% of the miles, for both their domestic and business needs.

An Economic Analysis of Twin Oaks

Twin Oaks is one of the best examples I know in the US of putting together all five aspects of my economic model for getting our needs met. Here's a quick look at Twin Oaks through that lens:

1. Things we currently define as needs that can be eliminated or significantly reduced.

---

community, but it still retains some of the early principles, including being strongly communal. Twin Oaks isn't the only community that was inspired by Skinner's work: Los Harcones in Mexico is another example of one of these still-extant communities.

[68] I've used these the raw numbers on p. 57 and US average statistics to derive the percentages in this book. Unless otherwise noted, the US average data is from a combination of the US Geological Service, the Environmental Protection Agency, and the Department of Transportation. Any mistakes in how that was done are mine. The stats came directly from the community. Twin Oaks is at a definite advantage in terms of being able to gather really good statistics because of its income and expense sharing set up. The community has just one electricity and water bill, for instance, so instead of self-reporting each individual household, they just sent me the summary of their community utilities as a whole. Their stats include agricultural activities for 50% of their food grown and, in the case of water and miles driven, also include their business activities. Finally, we estimated that Twin Oaks has, on average, 115 people on the property, including adults and children who live there and visitors and guests. Thanks to Sky Blue and Misty Vredenburg at Twin Oaks for their help in compiling and making sense of the data.

- Because the majority of members' work is a walkable commute (on the Twin Oaks property), the need for many cars is eliminated.
- Each member has a personal room—which is simply not a lot of personal space to fill with personal stuff. You could say that the physical choices have encouraged worldview choices; however you frame it, though, it means people just aren't accumulating a lot of stuff, and they are making choices regularly about what *not* to buy.

2. Things that can be shared, reducing the individual burden.
   - The community owns televisions and other "standard" recreational equipment, has a good-sized library, and has spaces for guests to sleep, group gatherings to happen, etc. No one individual needs to make enough money or invest in square footage for all of that in order to have access to it, nor do they need to individually own all that entertainment stuff.
   - Twin Oaks uses a "town trip" system, common among income sharing groups. One person collects a list of purchases individuals (as well as community entities like the kitchens) need and that person does the errand-running for everyone that day. This eliminates multiple car trips and a lot of human energy that most of us have to put in individually.
   - By collectivizing, Twin Oaks members can do things like put solar panels on their houses, have access to 450 lovely acres of land (with swimming ponds, walking trails, etc.), own tractors, and have things like a full, pretty good sound system for parties and concerts. Very few individuals can afford those kinds of amenities on their own.
   - Car sharing in particular makes a big impact on the community's collective ecological footprint and saves the community a lot of money. Beyond just town trips, there is also coordination of other travel.
   - Buying in bulk significantly reduces the cost of the staple foods they need to buy. Rice in a 50# bag costs less per pound than rice purchased in smaller quantities would, but you have to have a volume of eaters who can go through it before the moths find it.

3. Things that can be done for oneself (DIY, or do it yourself).
   - Here's where Twin Oaks really shines. They grow a significant chunk of their own food, a small team cooks meals for 100 people twice a day, they fix their own cars, tractors, and plumbing, and provide awesome childcare for their kids—all without laying out a bunch of money.
   - Twin Oaks is a bit of a collectivist aficionado when it comes to DIY entertainment: holidays like Validation Day (a tradition that has spread to multiple other intentional communities and involves creating handmade personal cards for each person in the community, celebrating what others enjoy and appreciate about them), as well

as simply epic parties for New Years, Halloween, and other celebrations, are highlights of the community's year. A lot of spontaneous fun also happens, reducing the desire for people to get off the farm to escape boredom.

4. Things that can be bartered or traded for.
   - At Twin Oaks, people record the number of labor hours they do, and if they do more than is required of them they can start to "bank hours." These hours can be traded as "Personal Service Credits," labor credits from your own labor balance given to another member to do a "personal service" for you, like build you a bookshelf, or give you a massage, etc. It's like an internal time bank.
   - The community also barters okara for pork sausage with a local pig farmer. Okara is a waste product from the community's tofu factory, and makes fine pig food.

5. Things that require money to acquire or get access to.
   - While Twin Oaks and its members certainly do operate in the regular US economy, the net result of all of the above is that they live on about $7,500 per person. That's just 26% of their county's average,[69] and represents a significant disconnection from the wider predatory economy, without living lives of deprivation.

Twin Oaks by the Numbers

Here are the raw numbers that I was given by Twin Oaks to use for this section of the book.

Water (all domestic, agricultural, and business):
   2014: 3,166,297 gallons
   2015: 3,046,338 gallons

Electricity used:
   2014: Total: 406,262 kWhs
   domestic: 270,494 kWhs
   business: 135,768 kWhs
   2015: Total: 405,674 kWhs
   domestic: 262,290 kWhs
   business: 143,384 kWhs

Electricity buy back from Solar:
   2014: 10,557 kWhs
   2015: 14,793 kWhs

Propane used:
   2014: Total: 18,102.44 gallons
   domestic: 9,200.76 gallons
   business: 8901.68 gallons
   2015: Total: 19,189.7 gallons
   domestic: 9,162.74 gallons
   business: 10,026.96 gallons

Car miles driven:
   2014: 241,046 miles
   2015: 283,468 miles

Landfill trash produced:
   1/1/2014-12/31/2014: 12.33 tons
   1/1/2015-12/31/2015: 14.66 tons

Average income for the adults:
   2014: $7,826
   2015: $7,043

---

[69] According to census data, the average per capita adult income in Louisa County, VA is $28,323. Twin Oak's per capita adult income was $7,826 in 2014 and $7,043 in 2015, averaging $7,435 for those two years.

Putting It All Together

So what happens when you put all of the techniques for getting your needs met together, in a coherent system? Even operating within the current big picture of horrible banking and trade practices, and swimming upstream against all kinds of cultural paradigms, by the liberal application of categories 1–4, Dancing Rabbit members live on an average of about $8,500 of annual income for the adults,[70] and Twin Oaks members on even less.

Obviously not everyone is going to move to a community like this, but one value of intentional communities is that we are like little social experimentation bubbles to try things out and see what is possible. I think the successes of places like Dancing Rabbit point to tremendous possibilities for what a reinvented economy might look like, providing principles (like my five approaches above) that can be applied in many contexts.

Another relevant number is that people at Dancing Rabbit work about 20 hours/week to meet their financial needs,[71] compared with 34.4 hours/week among average Americans, and 47 hours/week for full-time workers. That's a lot of life force saved by the judicious application of this model.

So let's play the "what if" game for a moment.

Dancing Rabbit and Twin Oaks members make less than $10,000 a year, so let's use that as the ballpark estimate of what's possible. The average American makes about $44K per year according to the World Bank. That means that we have two robust examples of community being able to bring your financial needs down to about 23% of the US average. If we needed only 23% of the money that we currently do, and then banking reform eliminated added interest, thus dropping our overall life costs by another amout, and then socialized medicine eliminated one of our most significant out-of-pocket expenses, and higher education was free…what then would the bottom line of our lives look like?

You can see how by putting together a holistic package of things—some personal, some communal, and some societal—we get to a place where a relatively modest universal basic income could cover nearly everything and lead to a very good life for far more people. I get excited about this because it represents a world where the pain of poverty could be eliminated at the same time that the worst of ecological crisis could be averted—both through the same holistic package of changes, all of which we have current access to.

So keep all of that in mind when we start talking about economic and legal system reform in the final chapter.

---

[70] It's important to note that Dancing Rabbit is in one of Missouri's poorest counties (Scotland) in a relatively cheap state to live in. Still, the average income in Scotland county is about $18,500, more than double what Rabbits live on.

[71] That number comes from an internal community survey done in April 2015.

Resilience and Security in the Age of Climate Disruption

Dorothy Day provides an excellent bridge between the fulfillment of needs, security, and community (from an unpublished manuscript quoted by Mel Piehl in *Breaking Bread: The Catholic Worker and the Origin of Catholic Radicalism in America* (Philadelphia: Temple University Press, 1982), pp. 99–100):

> Once we begin not to worry about what kind of a house we are living in, what kind of clothes we are wearing, we have time, which is priceless, to remember that we are our brother's keeper, and that we must not only care for his needs as far as we are immediately able, but try to build a bridge to a better world.

So what do the words "security" and "resilience" mean for us right now?

For me, these are closely related concepts. To be secure means to have your core needs met and to feel some degree of certainty that those needs will continue to be met. While it is questionable for a lot of people right now whether climate disruption and resource scarcity will allow us to ever have the kind of security many people enjoyed in the US for the last 50 years of the 20th century, there will always be more and less secure ways to set up our lives.

What is certainly true is that *resilience* will become more and more of a key component of security. Being resilient means that you can roll with changes as they come, with (relative) ease. A resilient system comes back to a place of equilibrium when it is thrown off. A resilient person is less likely to be thrown completely off-kilter by change and loss. A resilient community is one that provides for its members' needs and can change how it does so in response to the circumstances it and its members find themselves in.

I think of real needs as falling into two general categories: material needs (harking back to Henry David Thoreau: shelter, food, water, the ability to stay warm and cool enough; I'd add physical safety to this time-tested listed) and spiritual needs (which include love, companionship, purpose, and respect). All of these needs can be met in a variety of ways, and the fulfillment of those needs will look somewhat different for different people and (to some extent) within different cultural contexts: we all eat food, for instance, but the kinds of foods we eat, the staples of our diets and how they are produced and prepared, vary a lot from culture to culture.

Notice there are a lot of things I don't include that we take for granted in the US: ready entertainment, easy mobility, abundant personal space, a wide variety of (often imported) foods available at all times of the year, cheap gadgets and toys, fashion, and fast food. These are *not* essential to a feeling of real security; in fact, their pursuit can actually actively undermine a feeling of security. They *are* well aligned with a fast-paced lifestyle that defines success as material excess. And they are expensive to maintain, not only financially but also ecologically.

These things, while normal to Americans, are actually at cross-purposes with living a high-quality life.

We are going to have to learn to live without them. They are major contributors to climate change, pollution, and resource depletion. Imagine, for just a moment, your life without any of these things. It's hard to do for most of us, and each person probably has their personal hierarchy of what would be most hard to live without.

And yet, it's worth contemplating, because we have reached a place where we aren't going to have the choice to sustain all of this any more. And that means change. We can make change a friend or an enemy, largely dependent on our level of resilience.

Resilience is aided by some additional things beyond my list of core needs. Remember that I'm defining resilience as a measure of how easily you return to a state of equilibrium when things change. Certainly having basic skills like being able to grow your own food, and access to land to do it on, creates greater resilience than not having these things. Thus, I consider education to be one of the keys.

There are three types of education that I believe feed into resilience: skills development, understanding of history and culture, and being able to think critically and creatively. Essentially, this is a combination of hands-on, practical engagement with the physical world, and what gets labeled liberal arts. This combination is not likely to be found at a regular university, and in fact, there are probably only a handful of colleges in the US that do either of these really well.

Some examples of the hands-on piece are Warren Wilson in North Carolina and Sterling College in Vermont; for developing critical and creative thinking skills, I haven't seen anything better than tiny Shimer College in Illinois. Mostly I sense that this kind of education comes outside of the university environment. Street smarts should not be under-rated, nor should the usefulness of libraries and study groups with other people committed to real intellectual rigor. Spending time in sustainability-oriented intentional communities, on organic farms, and in indigenous communities might well be the absolute best education you can get. That's where truly useful skills-development seems most likely to happen at an accelerated rate.

The understanding of history and culture is also critical, because real resilience is aided by being able to get perspective on your situation. In some ways this means knowing enough to determine when to freak out and when to roll with it. Impending rise of fascism? Freak out; we've been here before, it happens in predictable patterns, and nothing good comes of it. Loss of all the perks of modern, fossil-fuel-intensive life? Don't freak out; we've been here before and it is actually a much more normal state of human life than what we have now—we can handle this. This perspective can make major changes easier to accept—humans have done this before, we can do it again. When we understand that the American normal is neither inevitable nor sustainable, we can have an easier time letting it go, and getting on with the new work in front of us.

This kind of education gives us tools for *discernment*. When we understand the context that we find ourselves in historically, politically, and ecologically, we are able to set new directions for ourselves. The people and places we are accustomed to looking to for guidance have actually never been through what we are about to go through. The well-worn path of least resistance (which is largely dependent on fossil fuels) may no longer be available to us soon. We need to understand ourselves, the basic skills of meeting our needs, and the context of both politics and ecology well enough to creatively set our own direction as individuals and communities.

Some of the definitions I found used interesting words to supplement the basic definition: toughness, and buoyancy. Toughness could imply having a thick skin, but I don't think that is the essence of it. I think it is more about a kind of vulnerability that keeps us from becoming brittle, and allows things to flow through you instead of shaking you. And buoyancy implies being able to float above things—to not get dragged in the undertow.

Both are aided by being able to get perspective on the situation at hand. In addition to knowing history, spiritual practices like meditation can help a lot with allowing us to get one foot outside the immediate crisis or upset and remember that this moment is not all that is. This is an example of having *emotional* understanding and tools that we need in order to stay both tough and buoyant. Emotional health is an incredibly important thing for us to invest in right now, though how we get there is going to look different for different people.

Physical health is equally important. Pain reduces resilience. And when our bodies are fully functional, we have more options for how to deal with change. One of the reasons that the healthcare crisis in the US is such a serious issue is that poor people have less access to resilience (and we have an increasingly large number of poor people in the US). Further, we've been sold a story for a long time that we do not know enough about our own bodies to do even simple medical things for ourselves. This strong reliance on experts has gotten us into an even harder situation: instead of learning about basic medicines and their safe use at home, we have given pharmaceutical and insurance companies that much more power to determine what kind of care our bodies get, based largely on their profits, and not our needs or empowerment.

Between the lack of training in emotional and basic physical healthcare, and the lack of accessible expert healthcare, we aren't arming ourselves very well as a culture for major transition. (It is also true that a loss of bodily resilience is a natural part of the aging process. As we get older, resilience becomes less about our physical being and more about our emotional and spiritual beings.) Our local communities can do a lot to change that, though. I've learned the basics of herbal medicine from other women I've lived with in multiple different communities, and having that knowledge and baseline confidence helps my sense of security as well as my family's resilience.

Emotional health is one of the biggest places that our culture has failed us—we get very little training and skills-building in basic emotional health. And it shows in our stats: according to the World Health Organization, nearly half of Americans (47.4%) suffer from some mental health disorder at some point in our lives, making us the least mentally healthy country in the world. Lacking basic self-esteem, and basic tools to handle change, many people sink into despair when their formerly stable reality changes. At a time when our realities are changing very quickly (not only because of climate change) we very much need to be able to roll with those changes, and most of us lack the ability to do so with any real ease. (I'll say a lot more about this in the next chapter.)

One of the key elements for building personal resilience is other humans. We need to learn from others, we often need help maintaining our health, and friends are incredibly important for dealing with emotional challenges. It is very difficult to be resilient in isolation, and yet that's what many people do when they are having a hard time—we isolate ourselves, afraid of being "a downer" or ashamed of what is happening inside us.

To be resilient, we need a strong dose of humility to ask for help, to be willing to pursue further learning (admitting that we don't now know what we need to know is a big step) and to risk admitting when our health is suffering. Part of why I am such a strong advocate for cooperative living is that it is much harder to hide out and isolate oneself in a community setting. (Not impossible: I certainly have lived with hermits in my time living in community. But even the hermits are more witnessed in their struggles, and most of them know they can reach out if they need to; sometimes just knowing that helps keep someone going.)

Another thing that draws us out and can help to keep us grounded is art. Lacking good emotional tools, often the only real release we get is through art, dance, and music. And artists are often very awake—they see and name what is out of balance and needs deeper looking into. Art is another way to gain perspective. Dance and music are cathartic for a lot of us. Being in the presence of art can help us be more resilient.

Angeles Arrien writes in *The Four-Fold Way: Walking the Paths of the Warrior, Teacher, Healer, and Visionary*:

> In many shamanic societies, if you came to a shaman or medicine person complaining of being disheartened, dispirited, or depressed, they would ask one of four questions.
> When did you stop dancing?
> When did you stop singing?
> When did you stop being enchanted by stories?
> When did you stop finding comfort in the sweet territory of silence?
> Where we have stopped dancing, singing, being enchanted by stories, or finding comfort in silence is where we have experienced the loss of soul.

Dancing, singing, storytelling, and silence are the four universal healing salves.

While I think it is important to not over-romanticize indigenous cultures, it is also important that, when your own culture is failing you, you look to other cultures for wisdom. It seems that this advice could be very potent for people seeking a more balanced and resilient way of living.

All of this means that we need to rethink what we mean by security and resilience. Security doesn't mean a big bank account, nor does it necessarily mean government-provided social safety nets or insurance policies. In a very fundamental way, security comes from growing our own food, collecting our water, and knowing our neighbors. Resilience comes from building our knowledge and perspective, having easily accessible social support of people who care about us, and finding tools that help us maintain a healthy state of being.

When you really know you are supposed to live cooperatively, and you really believe in the justice of that, you are going to start something wherever you go.

Brandy Gallagher, Founder O.U.R. Ecovillage

Chapter 4:
Starting a Residential Intentional Community

Starting the Transition Now, and the Power of Choice

I like choice better than not-choice. Most of us do. Choice is empowering, where being forced into something can be deeply disempowering. My basic take on where we are in the unfolding saga of climate disruption is that we are still, narrowly, in the window of choice when it comes to changing our lifestyles.

I'm writing this book in part to urge people to embrace choice while you can. Setting your own terms for how you do something like setting up an intentional community is always easier, and you are more likely to get more of what you really want and need if you pursue something deliberately. There is also a measured calmness to something you choose before the urgency really kicks in: if you have a few years now to gradually, thoughtfully unfold what a low-carbon life will be, that seems far better than having things start crumbling around you and acting from desperation.

Here are some good reasons to choose now:

1. The aforementioned calmness allows you to make better decisions.

2. Many groups adopt the philosophy of using some fossil fuels to get systems set up that will then be able to sustain themselves with little or no further fossil fuel inputs. That is only really possible while fossil fuels are still relatively cheap and easily available: at some point, that window will close.

3. Choiceful people are easier to live with than desperate people.

4. As fossil fuels become more expensive, you may find yourself more limited in terms of how far you can reasonably go to relocate. If your community dreams involve relocation, it might be good to do that soon.

5. Coming off a major loss is a bad way to start a relationship. As more people are directly impacted by climate change and economic desta-bilization, losses will become more common. Whatever resources you

currently have, it would probably be best to bring them to the table while you still have them.

6. Perhaps most compelling, the more time you have to establish systems and practice skills, the easier the transition will be for you and your group when things really do start coming apart. Given how long some of the social skills and cultural un/re-learning process can take, this is one of those things that it is best to get a jump on: five years of solid community skills-building under your belt might well be the best gift you can give your future self and those who depend on you.

I imagine you can think of more reasons to act sooner rather than later, but that gives you a flavor of the kinds of things I think about when I hear people wistful for community putting it off. Thus, my gloom-and-doom context for encouraging you to hop right on the intentional community train and start your projects now. The rest of this chapter is my guide to doing that well.

You Really Don't Want to Do This

I'm told that the most memorable 10 minutes of my "Starting an Intentional Community" workshop are the first 10 minutes. That's because I do my best to try to talk people out of attempting to start a new community as my first obligation to the movement. I also generally use the phrase "batshit crazy," which sticks in people's minds for some strange reason.

Why would I talk people out of it? I clearly want more communities in the world. (It's one of the main motivations of writing this book after all.) And I clearly think it can be done well. So why expend those minutes when people have presumably paid good money to hear me tell them they should totally do this?

Well, the main reason is that it is a little...well...batshit crazy. And I think part of the obligation of experienced people in any movement is to not sugar-coat the hard stuff. Speaking honestly builds trust and is just fair. So long as we are pairing that reality check with concrete support for those who decide to stick with it, this simply feels to me like the right thing to do.

So here's the gist of what I tell people, in hopes that a few of them will come to their senses and decide being a founder isn't for them—while a few others will strengthen their resolve and get a little more real about actually doing it.

Starting a community is a tremendous undertaking. I tell people it is like starting a small business, starting a nonprofit, getting married, and doing a really intense personal growth course all at once and all with the same group of people. I'm sure we can all think of people we'd be fine owning a business with, but would never marry. Or we are happily married (or partnered) but would never start a project, whether nonprofit or business with our beloved. Or we are fine with personal growth, but can't imagine mixing it with business. There's some real magic to getting the right people to do all this stuff with, and it is rare for it to really click.

It's like starting a business because you need to deal with the legal and financial stuff, and you really do need to be able to create a functional spreadsheet, do a good budget, market it appropriately, etc. We aren't talking Forbes 500 level business skills, but we are talking a basic package of business-type savvy and (perhaps harder to find in progressive alternative circles) a lack of resistance to doing all of this stuff.

It's like starting a nonprofit because in addition to basic business savvy, you also have to build support among fans (like donors, only they might be local decision-makers) and get and stay aligned around a mission and purpose that serves something other than profit and presumably is in the public good. Which also means having some discernment about what the public good is.

It's like getting married[72] because there are intense relationships involved that you have to be able to do well, and it is doubtful that you were taught those skills in public school or the competitive marketplace. If you have a hard time with one close relationship because your skills are not up to par, you will likely find that challenge multiplied in community, not diminished.

Finally, it is like a really intense personal growth course because that is actually what it is. I tell people that you shouldn't even bother trying to live in community (let alone start one) if you are not willing to approach it as one ginormous, lifelong personal growth experience. Generally, people who can't do that are the ones who have the worst (to the point of even traumatizing for some people) experiences in community. People who can do that fare a lot better.

(Please note that I am not saying you won't ever experience trauma in community if you are open to personal growth. Hard stuff happens all over, and bad behavior can manifest everywhere. What I am naming, though, is tendencies—the more you are willing to grow, the less likely something bad or hard that happens will be damaging to you in the long haul. This is true outside of community as well, but people often go into community with high expectations that bad stuff won't happen.)

Thus, when you add all of that up, it's a daunting thing, starting a new intentional community. But hey, if that sounds like fun to you, by all means, read on.

Some key things to consider when making a decision to be a founder:

- Should you start a new group or join an existing one? Many existing communities could really use new members. I generally advise, unless

---

[72] Depending on how you look at it, it might actually be worse or better than that. Some communities don't have missions that require as deep of a level of intimacy or engagement, and so for those groups, it might be not as intense as marriage. However, you can also think of this being a little like getting into a polyamorous relationship—less the sex—because you need to learn to relate functionally to a bunch of different people, all of whom have relationships with each other as well that complicate things.

you are wanting to do something really unique, or are wedded to a particular location where no groups currently exist, to seriously consider the relative ease of joining something instead.

The other reason to start something is that you may just be one of those people with a deep-seated need to start new things, and you'll simply chafe at being a joiner. If that is the case, then the world would benefit from your putting in the energy and time to do this. But do recognize that this is (at a bare minimum) a several-year commitment before you will have this thing landed.

- What motivates you to do this, both personally as well as a communally? The communal motivation is the easier question. Most people who start thinking about this are well aware that the options available to them in the wider culture aren't entirely working. That clarity of purpose will help you get started in designing your new project.

  What motivates you individually is often more subtle stuff. That said, it is really important to do the work of considering that, and to be brutally honest with yourself about it. Why? Because simple ego gratification, or wanting the title of founder isn't going to cut it. Being a founder is hard. You will encounter power dynamics with your group, and those will likely result, at least on occasion, in your being unfairly accused of something unsavory. You will not get exactly what you want in your community: either you will try to control that too strongly and push people away, or you will find that other people want things too, and they won't always match your personal desires exactly, and some compromise will be inevitable. And you will probably have to juggle a superhuman number of different roles, some of which you will inevitably be worse at than others, and either you or others may be hard on you about that.

  Ultimately, if your personal motivation for starting a community doesn't have a large dose of selfless service in it (and a connected willingness for humility and letting go), you are going to have a very rough ride. Better to do some serious soul-searching at the beginning and either decide to not do this, or prepare yourself as best you can for when it either isn't smooth sailing or doesn't go anywhere. And that soul-searching really will increase the chances of your project succeeding, and your getting a more communal and well-supported life out of all that effort.

- What will you get by starting a residential group, rather than a non-profit or small business?

  So many of us are drawn to community because we want to change the world, not just because we want a higher quality life than the one we can afford on our own. And that is especially true for founders. So it is worth asking if a residential project is really the best medium for your goals, or if you can do more good in the world via a business or nonprofit venture.

- Have you done adequate homework on this?

In this case, I mean things like reading *Communities* magazine,[73] talking to other founders to get their take on it, and visiting other intentional communities. I'm always amazed when people come to my workshops with plans on paper and maybe even a website up already and a Communities Directory[74] listing, thinking they are ready to start a community...but they've never actually set foot in a real intentional community before.

I not only recommend visiting communities, I specifically recommend visiting both ones that sound similar to what you are thinking you want and ones that *do not* sound similar. This is because reality and mental pictures rarely match up, and it is far better to find out that the things you thought you wanted really are what you want before you put a lot of time, energy, and money into starting something.

The opposite is also true—sometimes a community doesn't sound appealing at all on paper, but when you see and feel it in action, you discover something to love about it; thus my recommendation to also visit places that don't sound like a perfect match in theory. This can be especially good for potential founders to do because it will help you get clear both about what is essential to you, and what things you may be more flexible about than you thought you were.

My own story about that phenomenon is that when I first moved to community, I had an image of myself as someone who would just love to live in a cabin in the woods somewhere, pretty isolated and surrounded by the glories of nature. Shortly after moving to my first full-on community, my partner and I got a chance to do just that. It was great!

For about a week. And then I started noticing these strange longings to be right in the middle of things. I found myself very drawn to living in one of the dorms instead of our sweet little cabin, and resenting the 10 minute walk to home, pretty as it was. A few months later, we did a room swap and I was much happier after that. It makes me seriously cringe to think that I could have invested all those resources in starting a cabin in the woods-style community only to come to hate my own creation.

---

[73] *Communities* is available through the publisher, Fellowship for Intentional Community: www.ic.org/communities-magazine-home.

[74] The Directory offers free listings for communities (though donations are very much appreciated to keep this site going). You can look here to find communities to visit, see how other groups talk about themselves, and create a listing for a new project: www.ic.org/directory. You can also get a copy of the printed *Directory* from FIC. See previous footnote.

So one of the key rules for starting a community is: Know Thyself. And actual knowing takes *experience*, not just theorizing.

"Homework" can also be done at a group level if you are contemplating this with others. A social media group where you can share articles and resources with each other is a modern tool that can be really helpful with this. And taking a trip together to a communities conference is not only a fun way to learn, it also gives you an opportunity to get to know each other better. In the modern era of car obsession, a good ole road trip can go a long way to answering if you want to be a founder with these other folks.

So if you have answered the above inquiries and done your due diligence on research, then it is time to begin the process of starting a community. What follows is a general outline you can use to make sure you have your bases covered. The order of these items is rarely that important. Most important is that you don't neglect any of them.

Development Models that Can Work, and One that Doesn't

There are a number of approaches people take to starting a community. Here are some common models for groups getting started:

1. Someone has land and thinks, "It would be cool to have a community," and opens their land to others, retaining ownership of the property.

   When you have both land and a strong community urge, this can seem like a no-brainer, and indeed a number of successful communities have started this way. I don't however, recommend this. The power dynamics can be awful. Essentially this set-up is one where one person (or couple, or family) has the legal and financial power to be able to pull the rug out from under the rest of the group at any time. Whatever self-examination you have done up front about your motivation is great, but the bottom line is that if things start to feel bad or don't go in the way you'd like them to go, the temptation to back out (and take the land with you) is very, very strong, and you'd have the weight of the law behind you if you did.

   While that actually does happen sometimes, much to the heartbreak of everyone involved, what happens far more frequently is that people walk on eggshells around the owners, because they know perfectly well that this could happen at any time. It skews many conversations, and makes it very hard to cleanly and openly disagree with the owners. Expecting people to build community in a fully committed way under these circumstances is an unreasonable expectation.

   It is also a recapitulation of wider culture power-over dynamics where money determines how much say people have in their lives. If you doubt this is a real thing, think about presidential elections under Citizens United: it's kinda like that, but more up close and personal.

And while sincere people can still run for office and attempt good things, the whole dynamic can poison how people feel about the venture, sowing mistrust where it may or may not be warranted.

So, what to do if this is you? I strongly advise putting the land into a Land Trust as soon as possible. It is OK to start here, but make a firm commitment to sell the property to the group. It is OK (and wise even) to have mutually agreed upon milestones that need to be met before you turn over official ownership (such as having a certain number of people committed for a certain amount of time, and the group's having a reasonable business plan in place to be able to purchase it from you). And then follow through on it. Your follow-through will go a long way toward building trust and mitigating whatever weirdness might be there for people about having bought a piece of property that you have a longer (and probably deeper) relationship with than the rest of the group.

2. A group gets together based on people who are connected to each other and then generates answers to the basic questions about what the community will be and how it will operate together, before buying land.

This approach leads with social bonding. This can be a group of old friends, or people who know each other from school, or people who go to the same church. For communities that are primarily formed for deeper social connection, this can be fine. However, this one also comes with a warning label: it may be hard to get a viable vision and mission if you don't start with some degree of philosophical or mission alignment. In other words: this leads with friendship, but can be hard on the visioning process.

I've been part of four community start-ups (including my current one). The hardest one of those had three very close friends at the center of it—myself and two other women. We worked for several years to develop an urban ecovillage in Albuquerque, and we basically erred on the side of friendship rather than alignment. Mind you, we were aligned enough to be really close, and to have a great amount of faith in our ability to work things through together. (That last part proved to be true—but part of the working it out was two of us stepping out of the group and ceding the visionary leadership to the third partner.)

What we hadn't been clear about going into it was things like what development model we wanted to follow (I wanted to buy a property with pre-existing communal infrastructure, like an old monastery or school, with plenty of land, at the edge of town; another wanted to pick a block and start buying and renting properties and taking down fences) and what exactly we meant by "sustainable"—our definitions, once we got into it, were significantly different. Meanwhile, all three of us had brought other people into the group, talking up each of our versions of the community we saw…including our unexamined and undiscussed assumptions. That meant that when things fell apart, a lot of other people also got hurt.

So, lead with friendship if that's what is driving it. But don't expect to necessarily be able to do a grand vision. For that, you need to start with the vision and lead from there, *à la* the next option.

3. One person or a very small group has a basic vision and they invite others into that vision to put the more detailed flesh on the bones.

This one is much better if you do have things that are critical to you about the vision. It leads with vision and recruits only people with strong alignment with the concepts and plan. This decision allows you to do things that are a greater departure from the mainstream. To do something outside of the norm, you have to get everyone on board. If you are recruiting from a place of already having some clarity, that means you bring in only people who are willing to play at a similar level of radical. This will make your community decision-making process easier for the entire time you live together.

On the other hand, it can be hard on friendships. If you emphasize the mission over keeping any particular person in the group, people's feelings will almost certainly get hurt. If a dedicated member's lifelong friend gets excited about a community, but the group says no because the group has decided to car share and the friend just can't be OK with that, that's going to cause some real heartache. So just know that possibility going into this, and be prepared to have to make some hard choices in order to do the culture change work and to have the kind of community that is worth the investment of your precious life energy.

If you go this route, I strongly recommend keeping the initial decision-making group to no more than eight people. Others can be welcome to join the conversations, watch meetings, participate in social gatherings, etc. However, it is hard enough to make choices about the nature of the community with a group of that size, and in these early days, you will be answering some very fundamental questions. On the other hand, try to have at least three people involved at this stage (especially if two of them are a couple). Having more than one person doing this and thinking things through almost always leads to more viable answers, and to thinking about the most critical things.

Once you have the basics figured out (keep reading for what I think those are) then you can open it up and start actively recruiting more members (if the project is going to need more) based on what you've laid out.

4. After researching models and considering who, what, and where, a small, values-aligned group who like each other and have humbly

gotten some training move ahead with major decisions together. Research is essential. Learn as much as you can. Having at least one person in the group who loves research and loves pouring themselves into understanding something new is a great thing for a founding group. (Of course, having someone with significant prior community experience is another way to get that need met.)

Considering who, what, and where means being deliberative and consensual about things like what you are looking for in members, not only what the vision is but also what kinds of agreements will best support your vision, and the choice of the property.

The group size advice is the same as it was for the last category: keep it in the three to eight range until you've settled your basic framework. Again, you can have a larger interest group and invite others to come sit in on meetings, but in terms of who is actually making the decisions, it is better to limit that to a group that feels comfortably aligned with each other.

And finally, I'm recommending training: as much of it as you can afford and make time for. Training includes workshops on starting a community, professional support in thinking about what legal form(s) you are going to take, and especially social dynamics (this includes training in whatever decision-making model you are going to work with, conflict resolution, and basic communication). It's best to get at least some of that early on so that you have a clear, shared understanding of how you want to interact, and shared tools to work from.

This is the approach I think works the best, though #3 is also a common model that has a lot of successes associated with it, and if done carefully can definitely be done well.

The Basics: Vision, Decision-Making, and Membership Process
Community Visioning

There are many different techniques, approaches, and theories around visioning, and I'm not going to promote any specific one here because I think a lot of them have merit. The only guidance I'm going to give on that is that the sweet spot for visioning seems to be somewhere in the range of three to eight people: that gives you enough brains to chew on things from different angles, and not so many that you will struggle to get anywhere with it. It's harder with a bigger group because prior to visioning, the door is really wide open: anyone with a mildly radical or adventuresome streak might find themselves drawn to talking about starting a community, and that means there's a very wide range of what people might want to explore. Once your vision work is complete, you have narrowed the range of what is on the table, and making decisions with a bigger group becomes easier. But that first step is a bugger with a big group.

So beyond that, use whatever process you feel drawn to, someone in the group has experience with, or your facilitator or consultant recommends, and make the process work for you. I want to emphasize instead in this section some of the things I believe groups need to think about and include at some point during whatever process you decide to use.

First, in general you need to be willing to lose individuals in order to lay a shared foundation to build a solid group. It is far better to discover your misalignments during the visioning process than after you've moved in together.

Make sure that you clearly articulate shared values in the process. Your values will become the foundation you use for your decision-making. Decision-making is really tough without an articulation of your values: without them, group process is a free-for-all, and the tendency is for the group to drift quickly away from whatever the original vision was.

The following words are ones that I consider to be problem words in a vision statement:

Sustainable/Sustainability
Community
Safety/Safe/Safely
Respect/Respectful
Affordable
Diversity/Diverse
Sharing

These words are problematic because they simultaneously don't mean much and can mean radically different things to different people...all of whom will have a tendency to read their preferred meaning into them. And that's a major problem, because sometimes those discrepancies don't emerge until years down the road, when everyone is heavily invested in the vision they have of the community and they find themselves in deep conflict with their community mates. Often people feel really betrayed, even though this particular mistake, as best I can tell, is almost always innocent.

These particular words are also very popular: they appear in most communities' vision statements, and yet the manifestations of them vary almost as widely as the housing options in community. For instance, does "sustainable" mean that the group is committing to recycling and having bike racks in the parking lot? Or does it mean you share cars and have rigorous goals around carbon emissions that supercede other desires in decision-making?

Same with "community." With that word, someone will picture a full-on commune while someone else is picturing the nice neighborhood of their childhood where neighbors fed them cookies after school. And "affordable"? Does that mean that someone of average income in the city can afford to buy a house or that the group has committed to being permanently affordable to people, say, living on disability? There's a huge difference between those, and yet both are reasonable interpretations of the word.

"Safety" is even worse, because it can actually mean polar opposite things. For one person, safety means never being around raised voices, and for another it means being accepted...even when they raise their voice in the heat of the moment. (Oh, wait...did safety even refer to emotional safety, or were we talking about physical safety...? Ufdah!)

It's OK to include these, but just make sure to define them enough that you don't leave these kinds of massive ambiguities unresolved. Also, be on the lookout for other words that might arise in your particular process. Less common and equally problematic words include *spiritual, justice, acceptance, tolerance, stewardship,* and the ever-popular adjectives, *reasonable* and *authentic.*

Sometimes people think it is better to wait until you have a bigger group to do your visioning, but it is hard for people to put in the energy to start a community when they don't really know what they are joining. So be bold and honest and draw a clear circle around what you want. Do enough so that people know clearly what they are joining, and not so much that there is no space for new ideas and initiative.

What that translates into concretely is probably about one to three pages of text: a paragraph is too short to effectively communicate what you are about. It is likely that if you go over three pages, you are probably both over-thinking and over-determining.

One more tip for visioning: try answering the questions on the online version of the Communities Directory (at ic.org/directory/new-listing). If your group members can comfortably answer most of them (and you give the same answers!), plus give a list of shared values, you are probably comfortably on the same page with the community vision.

Membership Process

A key question in determining what your membership process should be is this: how intimate and aligned does your vision require you to be? Diana Leafe Christian (author of the now-classic *Creating a Life Together: Practical Tools to Grow Ecovillages and Intentional Communities*) talks about the strong relationship between decision-making, membership process, and vision.

While I've come to talk about this in terms a little different from Diana's, her recognition of that relationship was insightful and got me started down this track. My basic summary of that is this:

The *less mainstream* your vision, the more careful you need to be that prospective members actually understand and are willing to commit to it. Thus, you need a more thorough vetting process.

The *more intimate* your vision is, the more you want to choose people as if you are getting into a committed relationship with them. Intimacy may mean any number of things, and the most common of these are doing lots of personal growth work together, income sharing, and/or having more limited personal space.

The *more alignment* your decision-making system calls for the more carefully you need to screen people for both vision alignment and willingness to do their own work to meet others where they are at. Thus, consensus requires more diligent screening of members than a simple majority voting system: you do not want to find yourself in a consensus process with someone who doesn't listen well, can only stubbornly hold to their own ideas, or can't recognize others' needs as being as legitimate as their own. Communities with a sole decision-maker can get away with being even more loose.

So given that very general guidance, I'd say the basics of a good membership process are:

A clear timeline for how long it usually takes. I know groups who have a three-month "provisional" membership period, and groups whose process can take up to four years to become a full member. I think a year is a good length: as people at East Wind used to say when I lived there, "Anyone can fake it for nine months—a full year is a lot harder." And I think there's some truth in that. See a person through the full turn of the year, through their favorite and least favorite season, and through enough time that the rose-colored glasses and "on my best behavior" thing can both fade, and you'll have a much better sense of whether they are someone you want to live with.

A clear process for them to follow. Don't spring surprises on people, and do lay it out at the beginning so there are no misunderstandings. If they need to attend four meetings, tell them that. If they need to read your process manual or take a workshop on your conflict resolution process, tell them that. This implies, of course, that you have done the work as a group to get clear about how someone becomes a member.

Provide mentorship and other support. Moving into a community is a big transition. It is different culturally at the very least, and is often also different economically and ecologically. Don't expect them to figure it out for themselves, and do provide both informational and emotional support for this transition. Also, don't skip this if someone has lived in another community before: they may not be learning cooperative living for the first time, but they may have assumptions based on how their old community did things that can lead to unintended misunderstandings.

A matter-of-fact feedback process. Living together means receiving feedback, and acclimating people to that reality early on is a really good idea. Also, if they can't handle getting feedback, they probably aren't ready for living in community. I've watched a lot of people come into community for the first time where my initial impression was that it was never going to work... only to be pleasantly surprised that they did so well with feedback that, by the time the decision to accept them rolled around, it was easy to honestly say yes to them.

A process for current members to talk through concerns about a potential member with each other. Some groups do this in a closed session, and others invite the potential member to come to that session. There is merit in both choices, but either way it is important that members be able to talk openly about both concerns and enthusiasm for the new person. It is also important that it be OK for people to use both their intuition and intellect in that conversation. You don't want to stop at, "I have a bad feeling about this" or "I'm not comfortable around this person" but being able to voice that as a starting place can often lead to deeper understandings for both the speaker and the whole group. If the person isn't present, it is important to give them a summary of any concerns that were raised and give them a chance to respond.

Clear and even-handed criteria for membership. This implies both assessment criteria and decision-making criteria. This could be as simple as following your usual consensus process, or it could be very specific to membership. For instance some groups say there have to be both no objections to the person and at least X number of people who are really excited about the person. This avoids a case where a person will find themselves joining a community where everyone is lukewarm about them and not really find any strong friendships—a situation that is not very good for anyone. Those excited people play a really important role in orienting and acclimating people who are new. It's hard to put that energy in when you simply aren't excited about them.

As far as assessment criteria, I think there are three main categories you need to be mindful of:

1. Ability: Can they fulfill the requirements of membership?

2. Alignment: Are they aligned with the vision and with current agreements?

3. Social skills: Have they demonstrated an ability to be a good group member in terms of their social savvy?

Here's a breakdown of each of these:

1. Ability: Can they fulfill the requirements of membership?
   Assessment type: Self
   The group's responsibility for this one is to both be clear about what you need from new members, and to communicate that thoroughly. People can only self-assess well if they know what the bars are. This one includes any financial and labor contributions required, and may also include anything else you believe is essential to be a fully participating member. Here are some examples of the kinds of things you may put on that list, depending on the nature of your community:
   - attendance at meetings
   - tolerance of lots of kid energy
   - any spiritual practices you require
   - willingness to do conflict resolution using tools the group has agreed on

- letting go of their personally owned vehicle
- living in the type of housing the group has available
- building their own home
- supporting themselves in the environment you are in
- being on email regularly
- keeping public spaces clean to the group's standard.

In other words, those additional requirements can be anything that is central to how your group is set up (or anticipates being set up). Once this information has been thoroughly communicated to a potential member, then I think it is best to let them self-assess.

2. Alignment: Are they aligned with the vision and with current agreements?
   Assessment type: Self and Community
   As with the last one, the community has an obligation to share your vision and basic current agreements with the potential member and ask them to self-assess. Some of this will almost automatically have already happened—for some reason this person was drawn enough to your group to be hanging around and taking an interest. That's a good first step, but it isn't enough.

   The tricky part here (and why I recommend the community playing a role in this and not just leaving it up to the person) is that community members know a lot more than the prospective about what it actually means to be aligned. Someone can think to themselves that they are really all in for sustainability, but may not actually understand that this means they might not be able to just drive wherever they want, or buy that junk food they spend their whole visitor period sneaking out to buy because they hate the food and are too polite to say so. Members will discern things from behavior and how the person talks about themselves, their aspirations, and even the community itself that the community is smart to not ignore. Make it a conversation, but try to help people be more honest (and aware) than they might be on their own about whether they really are aligned.

3. Social skills: Have they demonstrated an ability to be a good group member in terms of their social savvy?
   Assessment type: Community
   Here's where things get sticky. We pretty much hate passing judgment on each other in the communities movement, and for good reason: we have all experienced the sting of someone judgmentally writing us off, or shutting us out of something because, on some level, they have found us unworthy. And it is especially hard when your assessment and theirs don't match up. This is painful and can be destructive to relationship, sometimes even causing material harm to

the person on the receiving end if it involves loss of a job or partnership, for instance.

One of the challenges as we mature and start seeing the world in more subtle terms is learning to distinguish between discernment and judgment. Judgment has at its core a diminishment of the person's worth. It says that there is something fundamentally wrong with the person or the action, and is therefore almost always arbitrary to some degree: it is based on one moral framework and not another that we use to stand above someone else and judge them. Judgment is not what we want. We do, however, want and need discernment.

I think of discernment as being the ability to assess whether someone's actions or intentions are a match for the goal at hand. It is non-arbitrary: we have deliberately come up with some goal, and we are looking whether or not we are on the same page about that goal and our commitment to it. It has nothing to do with the person's value—what isn't aligned with one goal can be perfect for the pursuit of another.

Our community vision is a big goal, and allowing people into the group who are simply not aligned with that vision is the road to eroding the group's ability to fulfill that vision.

Cooperative culture is a fundamental underpinning of any cooperative endeavor, including a residential community. So when I am saying groups should use their discernment and actively assess whether someone has the skills at the time they apply for membership to contribute productively to a community, it is about applying discernment. And the *community* needs to be the one to make this assessment.

Laird Schaub has a great articulation[75] of what those traits and skills are, and it is a longer and more nuanced list than you might think. I've taken Laird's list and broken it into two sections, skills that I think are basic and ones that I think are more advanced:

Basic skills:

How well can you articulate what you're thinking?

How well can you articulate what is happening to you emotionally?

How comfortable are you sharing emotionally with others?

How completely and accurately do you hear what others say?

How easily can you shift perspectives to see issues from other viewpoints?

In a meeting, how easily can you track where we are in the conversation?

How well do you understand your own blind spots and emotional triggers?

How open are you to receiving critical feedback?

---

[75] Quoted from Laird's communityandconsensus.blogspot.com blog entry of January 26, 2009.

Advanced skills:

How easily can you see ways to bridge different positions?

Are you able to show others that you "get" them?

How well can you read non-verbal cues?

Can you readily distinguish between Process comments and Content comments?

How adept are you at approaching people in ways that put them at ease?

How well do you understand the distribution of power in cooperative groups?

Do you have a healthy model of leadership in a cooperative group?

How do you respond in the presence of emotional upset and conflict?

Can you distinguish between projection and what's actually happening in the moment?

Are you more interested in understanding than being understood?

In a category of its own:

How interested are you in getting better at the above?

Now, mind you, no one is going to be terrific at all of these, but if people are missing more than a couple of the items I've placed on the "basics" list, that's not a good sign. My point in reprinting Laird's list is to give you a sense of what kinds of things you are looking for. In some ways, the very last question is the most critical: are they not just willing-if-you-make-them but actually interested in learning?

Given that the most common cause of intentional communities' failing is a lack of strong enough social skills, this last member criteria may well be the most important one.

Decision-Making

The decision-making model your group uses will be a big determiner in the feel and function of your group. This is one of the single most impactful decisions you'll make. My general advice is to base this decision on three things: what will best empower your vision, what kind of culture you want to create, and how willing and interested in training you are. (Note: I'm addressing my comments here to groups that do not have a single, charismatic leader, but rather are seeking something more democratic in their approach.)

The easy default is to use a voting system: it's familiar, requires little or no training, and you can pull out Robert's Rules, that time-tested document for how to run meetings.

The big drawback to voting is that it is familiar and easy precisely because it is well-aligned with our current cultural paradigm of competition and independence: in other words, choosing voting means you are surrendering one potentially very powerful leverage point for culture shift. Voting systems are problematic for the same reasons that our current political system is problematic: it will encourage camps, and discourage real listening.

This is really simple mechanics: once you have secured enough support for a proposal to pass it, there's really no need to take the rest of the group into account. My take on voting systems within community is that they create an inherent contradiction that your group will likely struggle with the whole time you live together: where community is about care and deliberation, voting is more about expediency and winning, and those two things are not really the same things at all.

To get a bit more concrete, in any given vote, nearly half the people in your group can be deeply unhappy about the outcome and still have the decision be "legitimate." Now this might not be a big deal if the decision isn't a very important one. However, I think we get into community for substantive reasons, and that means the things we are discussing and deciding upon will be similarly substantive in many cases. Having to live with what you consider to be bad decisions on things that matter in a very intimate setting, and having to live with the people who made that decision over your objections, is not a good set-up. It breeds perceptions of being misunderstood and uncared for, especially if you start to get camps forming and your camp is smaller than the winning one.

That's ugly enough in national politics: at the far more personal level of neighbors, it feels even worse.

The most common choice communities make is to use consensus, and I think that's a really good choice, IF your group is willing to get some good training and see consensus as a skill set that is worth cultivating over the long term. Simply doing what I call "consensus mechanics" over top of a competitive culture framework is not a good idea: it can in fact be far worse than voting, which at least is honest disempowerment.

It is worse because we expect more of each other when we do consensus: we expect to be heard and taken seriously, to not be belittled or argued down. While you can certainly have respectful dialogue in a voting system (there are better and worse manifestations of voting for sure) the fundamental paradigm it is built on has limits in terms of how much respect you need to give other people's perspectives, and at some point you can just shrug and say, "whatever."

The bad thing that happens when you try to combine consensus mechanics with competitive culture is that people will feel obligated to act as if they are listening, but their responses will be competitive, argumentative responses, they will take what you say and use it against you, and if you try to use your blocking power to stop something from happening, you'll get tremendous pressure to not get in their way. Please note, I'm not saying people do this on purpose: I'm saying that this is the cultural paradigm we've all been taught to follow—it's how you win in our culture. And those dynamics can't help but come into our meetings.

Consensus isn't about winning: it is about getting bigger than your personal perspective and finding a way for all of us to care not only about each other, but about the purpose that brought us together. In this case, that is the group's mission. And that is also the underlying theme of sustainable cooperative culture: deep care for the whole, and sense of purpose.

In consensus, we have two simultaneous goals: make a good decision (with "good" being determined by how well it aligns with the group purpose and good of the members) and strengthen our relationships with each other. Good voting systems also ideally do the first one: come to the best decision. But when it comes right down to it, relationship is often collateral damage in voting, and for most people that's expected and accepted.

I think we can do better than that, and part of why I advocate for consensus is that I think (when it is done skillfully) it is a lot better. That said, it's also a pain in the ass, especially in the learning process, when competitive culture patterns will inevitably emerge, despite your best cooperative intentions.

Learning to do both of these things at the same time is a major undertaking, and the reason I recommend training. Some of the key skills of good consensus training are:

- Learning to listen for agreement, and for how different ideas enrich (rather than detract from) each other. Cultivating genuine curiosity, particularly in the face of disagreement.

- Learning to listen "under" the positions (what someone thinks we should do) for the values (what is important to the person) and bridge from there, and finding the connection between personal collective values.

- Increasing our skills in both giving and comfortably hearing emotional and intuitive input.

- Working on assuming the good intent of others, again, especially when we disagree.

- Learning to distinguish between being heard and being agreed with; between having input and getting your way.

- Practicing making our input for the group good, rather than solely for personal gain.

Those skills make a huge difference to having a functional culture around your consensus process. I'll say a lot more about culture in the next chapter, and a big section of *The Cooperative Culture Handbook* is dedicated to building these kinds of skills.

The other requirement for consensus to be functional is being aware of a few key mechanics. These are:

- Sequencing your conversation to best get input prior to starting to problem solve.

- Not allowing blocks based on personal preferences or values that aren't shared.

- Having your facilitators hold three things as prime directives: curiosity about differences and concerns, collective creativity in problem solving, and awareness of shared values and mission.

Here's a brief exploration of each one:

- **Sequencing.** The biggest mistake consensus groups make is doing things in an unproductive (and ultimately time-sucking) order: they go to proposals too soon. Some groups actually require that you start with a proposal, and won't let people bring something up unless they've already thought about what they want the group to do about it. There are two main problems with this: it makes a farce of input, and it causes people to get invested in a particular idea before they have any basis for knowing if it is really going to work for the whole group, almost guaranteeing conflict.

  It makes a farce of input because the proposer has already drawn a box around what is acceptable to talk about. It's like building a house on top of a half a foundation: if anyone else tries to add a foundational piece at this stage, no matter how much it is needed to shore the house up, it's going to be awkward,

  The core of good consensus process is the input phase. If you first get from people what their input is (meaning what is important to them or concerning for them about the topic) then you have what you need to start building a proposal.

  You have to be absolutely disciplined about this: starting problem solving and proposal generation before everyone who has a say in the decision gives their input means you aren't playing with a full deck. And if you start that construction process prematurely, you will have to backtrack, or risk losing people's consent. This squeezebox is often acutely felt by the people whose input would have generated a different proposal. The facilitator will often think they are doing a good thing by encouraging people to just debate the proposal at hand, and not wander "off topic." However, what this does is essentially muzzle the people who never really had a chance at authentic participation.

  And that's why I say getting the sequence wrong just about assures you of having conflict. While some people are pretty good at putting out an idea and not being very invested in it, a lot of people aren't good at that. If they voice their idea too soon, they will start building attachment around it, and then it's going to be a fight. It's even worse if a whole committee has spent time on it—they will reinforce whatever attachment is there. It also runs the risk of the creator(s) of the proposal experiencing a sense of rejection, and concluding they just wasted a bunch of time because when it came to the group it wasn't "good enough for the group."

The truth is that it isn't good enough, but that's not the proposer's fault: it's the process's fault.

This dynamic is a major contributor to the "consensus takes forever" complaint that often gets leveled at us advocates. My response is: yep, *bad* consensus takes forever. Good consensus takes just as much time as you need for real buy-in from the group, which makes implementation far easier.

That's where the time savings comes in: if you do the process well, it might actually take you less time to go from your first conversation to satisfactory implementation. You also save time in the really big picture, because your decision-making isn't creating more conflict that needs to get painstakingly worked out at a later date. You have to think of this as a whole system, where the group culture, your decision-making, and the health of your relationships can either positively feed each other, or negatively drag each other down. What I'm laying out in this book is a culturally coherent package that does that.

- **Testing for legitimate blocks.** This is the second critical thing for functional consensus: you need to have a concept of "legitimate block." Many groups err in letting people block for any reason. Those reasons run the gamut from caring about the group health and tending to the group purpose, to having a personal concern that feels so big you can't say yes, to grinding an ax that has nothing to do with the subject at hand. If you have no way to legitimize a block, the group purpose will get gradually dumbed down under the weight of these latter two categories: personal philosophy and personal baggage.

  This is the reason I emphasized having articulated group held values in the section on visioning: if you don't know what your shared values and purpose are, you have no protection against frivolous blocks (or frivolous arguments, regardless of what your decision-making process is).

  Not only do communities make this mistake, but social change organizations of all sorts can fall prey to this. I worked with a couple Occupy groups during the heyday of that movement, and this was a huge problem for them: they cast the net so wide in terms of values that their attempts at consensus regularly got thwarted by people who came in without a real understanding of what they were trying to do, and the process let them do it.

  I recommend a process something like this:

  When someone blocks, ask the person to articulate the reason for the block, and how it is connected to a group-held value. Ask the rest of the group if folks can see the connection to that group-held value.

(Note, this does not mean that the person who says they see the connection agrees with the blocker, it just means they get the connection.) Depending on the size of the group, there should be some threshold of people who can see how it relates to the group-held value. (So for instance, for a group of 10, that might only be one other person; for a group of 60, you might require four people affirming the block.) Finally, the group should ask the question, "Are there worse consequences for accepting this block or not accepting it?" and weighing that as a group, again referencing your group-held values. Only if the block is affirmed by enough people and is deemed to be less negatively impactful on the group is a block considered to be legitimate.

- **Having your facilitators know their stuff.** Facilitating a consensus meeting is not the same thing as following Robert's Rules, and it is much more than simply calling on people. My mentor, Laird Schaub, has developed a two-year Integrative Facilitation training that teaches this skill set; doing it well is just that complicated, and requires that kind of deep commitment to learn. So I know I am only scratching the surface in the next few paragraphs, but it seems important to say something about the most core things a facilitator should be keeping the group on track with: curiosity about differences and concerns, collective creativity in problem solving, and awareness of shared values and mission.

  The third, awareness of shared values and mission, means simply holding in the back of your mind what I've just described related to group-held values, and remembering to go through that process if things get confused or heated.

  The first one is the most essential attitude of consensus: genuine curiosity. No one thinks just as we do, and no one has an identical set of experiences and knowledge to bring to the group. That's a good thing about groups, and it is also a hard thing: we *will* disagree with each other. How a group handles the moment of disagreement is the best predictor for how solidly they understand cooperative culture. Do we try to talk each other out of our different perspectives, and turn it into an intellectual competition? Or do we get curious, wanting to understand how the other people got where they did and what they have to bring that is interesting and enriching for us? The facilitator's most important job is to model that curiosity, and then model doing something productive with what came from it.

  Which leads to the other thing I like to see facilitators do: hold space for creative problem solving. Really good problem solving takes everything of real merit that was said in the input-gathering phase, mixes in the group-held values and purpose of the group, and essentially makes them into criteria for a good solution. The facilitator's job is then to help the group work together in good faith and creativity to find the best match between those criteria and the real world of limitations and opportunities the group is dealing with.

Often, a consensus-oriented facilitator will be the first to spot how to put the elements together, because we learn to be agreement-prejudiced as we are training. However, that's not really the facilitator's job: their job is to support the group in their creativity and discernment about what solutions actually fit those criteria.

As a starting place, groups that work on the things I have listed here will have a much higher rate of success in actually implementing consensus. And those groups will reap the benefits in seeing their culture shift and deepen into being more cooperative and more authentically nurturing for their members.

One final note: a number of groups use some hybrid of voting and consensus. While I'm not a big fan of "modified consensus" (I think the problems you are trying to solve with modifications are often best solved by better training in the cultural aspects of consensus) I do think that a group making some decisions as a full group by consensus and then having a democratically elected village council that operates by consensus is a fine model, especially as groups get bigger. Both Dancing Rabbit and Twin Oaks use a variation on the council system.

I think the bottom line has to be: do what works for your group. Don't let yourselves off the hook for getting properly trained and working on your culture; do get creative about how exactly you put this together. Make it yours.

The Complex Topic of Diversity

Intentional communities form for a particular purpose, and that purpose becomes the prime directive in decision-making. Membership is no exception to that. Some community purposes will have a very clear and obvious tie to wanting a lot of "diversity," and some won't. However, how much and what types of diversity you have is an important question for every community to talk about.

That said, this question gets tricky in part because we use this word now to cover a heck of a lot of territory, and in doing so, we often get ourselves into trouble. So I am going to distinguish between three different categories of diversity (among many that could be named) and then take them one at a time: diversity of thought and style; diversity of identities; and diversity in impacts on the group.

- **Diversity of thought and style** means that none of us think, act, and speak in quite the same way as others. So long as someone's philosophy is not actively in tension with the group's purpose, this kind of diversity is positive and needful in groups. A group working on sustainability or economic justice issues, for instance, will benefit from lively debate about how to approach those things. But too much difference that is too strongly clung to can be a problem.

For instance, if the group hasn't settled the question of how techie you want your sustainability to be, and one person is adamant that the only sane approach is full use of modern tech while another is equally adamant that hand tools are the only thing you can count on when things collapse, that's too much diversity from stubborn folks to be able to manage. It is not the diversity, but rather the lack of social skills that can make philosophical differences too much—however, simply having a difference (again within the range of the group's mission) isn't itself a problem. Similarly, style differences mean that we have a variety of ways to get at a topic, or to connect with neighbors, new people, and each other. It can be frustrating at times, but overall makes the group stronger.

Please note that if you have settled some question (like the tech question above) it is fine to have only members who align with this. Are you eliminating diversity? Yes. And you should not be afraid to do so when it comes to diversity within this category.

- **Diversity of identities** is an almost entirely positive thing. *So long as you don't treat your community like a mini-melting pot where differences are expected to melt away in the soup of the group,* race, class, gender, sexual orientation, and ability differences (to name a few) lead to rich environments. Do they sometimes also lead to challenges? Yes. Just as the wider culture is remarkably disintegrated and laden with tensions around all of these issues, in community too they bring up very real challenges to be grappled with. But we need to be able to work through these kinds of challenges in order to be a movement that works for everyone. The more types of diversity you have in your group early on, the better job you will do with creating structures that are not unconsciously off-putting or downright oppressive.

If you look around a few years into the community formation process and realize you are pretty monocultural in one of these areas, be active in asking yourselves questions about why, and don't wait for a real human being to show up who is of the currently unrepresented identity and expect them to do your work for you on this. There are plenty of resources out there readily accessible to help a group work on diversity issues (some of which I list in the Resources Appendix), and I encourage communities to avail themselves of those resources.

Finally, a quick note on age diversity. Most groups want this and benefit tremendously from having it. And we are all aging, so the issues that come with an aging population are going to be part of what we grapple with if our communities last for any length of time. Thinking seriously about aging in place before the first person needs it is a smart thing to do. You also want to talk about where the lines are between individual responsibility, community responsibility, and family responsibility (for those who have family).

Income sharing groups are the most likely to assume community responsibility for their members' aging in place, but it isn't an automatic thing. If you don't talk about this prior to someone's health starting to go downhill, you may find yourselves in a very awkward position of needing to talk logistics, money, and medical philosophy at a time when someone is feeling incredibly vulnerable, and may well think they've been abandoned if other people in the group were not also assuming that elder and hospice care was part of what they signed up for.

- **Diversity in impacts on the group** is the hardest one in some ways. Some things are just too much for a group to handle. It's one matter if your group purpose is explicitly to work on or experiment with these areas. In that case you are obligated to deal with them. However, if you aren't, there are a few categories where courting too much diversity can really swamp the group. These are primarily in the number of children a group has, and the number of people with serious mental illnesses and addictions you have. These may seem to be in direct contradiction to what I was saying above, but both of these involve particular nuances that make them different in real life.

The child issue is a bit more straightforward. I've heard rumor of communities with more children than adults, the most extreme of which was about 70% people under the age of about 15. To put it bluntly, we all like the sound of *It Takes a Village*, but it is hard to not get *Lord of the Flies* if the kid population swamps the adult population that extremely. It can work: IF the main purpose of the community is very child-oriented. But if it isn't, the kid energy can take over and make it really hard to make progress on whatever else the community wants to be working on.

So this is a question of balance more than absolutes: almost all groups want children. They bring life and spontaneity into a place in an incredibly valuable way, and we want to be welcoming to people who have children. So this isn't about "no kids" in most cases—it is about having some attention on making sure there are enough adults on the scene to reap the benefits of the *It Takes a Village* concept. Some groups actually have a kid ratio that they try to maintain, something like wanting to keep it around no more than 25% kids. That ratio helps take the pressure off the parents without other people (who may or may not like hanging out with children: you get both) feeling overwhelmed or burdened by other people's choices.

So my advice on this is simply to think about it and be deliberate.

The mental illness issue is even harder. The tension between wanting diversity of identities and the problems this form may cause is even stronger: there is mounting evidence that both mental illness and addictions have a very strong biological component. A case could be made that one can't help their mental health status any more than they can control what gender they were born into or their sexual orientation. And I'm willing to grant that.

The difference in my mind, though, is whether a group can responsibly and compassionately handle people's needs who are living with mental illness and addiction. I'm not talking about minor mental health struggles: we are all on that spectrum somewhere, and modern life seems to make it worse for nearly all of us. I'm talking about the more serious manifestations of deeper, more constant struggles. If your group has the skill and energy to work with this, then great—take it on, and know you have the gratitude of many people for doing that important work. If you can't though, I strongly encourage groups to figure out how much they can handle and not go past that point. (Note: "how much" may mean both severity of the challenges, and the percentage of people in the community with those challenges.)

The thing is, community is a very rough place for people who may be triggered into self-harming patterns by too much intimacy, too many people being in their businesses, too many new faces too frequently (if you are a community that has a lot of visitors), and too much pressure to perform well in terms of communication and social dynamics. And if the group doesn't have the skills, compassion, and patience to know how to actually help, it isn't a kindness or a responsible thing to invite people in with these kinds of struggles.

In fact, this is a place where good intentions can go very, very awry. For people struggling with their mental health, community may be more supportive, but it is rarely more *safe*. And I have seen too many instances where someone had a breakdown of some sort, and the community tried really hard to handle it themselves, which only delayed the person getting the professional support they needed. In some cases, that made it much, much worse.

So here's my recommendation: take this really, really seriously and self-assess as a group painfully honestly. This isn't about rejecting people because they are damaged, flawed, or bad; it isn't really about them at all. It is about communities being realistic about what you can responsibly handle.

I predict that this is going to become a much bigger deal as economic and ecological collapse progresses: we are all moving into a less stable era that is likely to create more challenges in this arena, not less. And everyone needs community: people with mental health issues are no exception. I'd love to see more communities go the route of getting the training needed to be responsible homes for people who are falling apart. I'd also like to see more communities (or organizations using community as a tool) embrace this *as* their mission. But if that isn't you, then please don't pretend it is.

Similarly, if you are someone with serious mental health struggles who is drawn to community, I strongly advise picking your group very carefully, and vetting the community just as deliberately as I'm suggesting all communities vet all of their potential new members. To go back to the marriage analogy: you deserve a spouse who is going to non-judgmentally and very concretely support who you actually are, rather than some fantasy of normative psychology. Not all groups are going to be able to pull that off, but some can for sure.

How Do You Deal With Conflict?

Conflict happens all the time. It is unavoidable, especially when we enter into meaningful relationships with each other meant to create something powerful for us. None of us thinks in identical ways to others, none of us communicates in a way that is comfortable and perfect for every other person, and all of us are carrying baggage that can cause us to be less than fun to be around at times. We humans are imperfect, messy creatures, and we've not been taught well how to navigate conflict when it arises.

One of the unfortunate outgrowths of all of that: few of us have really positive experiences with navigating conflict, and so most of us are conflict-avoidant to some degree or another. We go into community with high hopes for a better life, and those hopes can easily feel dashed when conflicts emerge.

The good news is that, just like cooperation, conflict management and resolution skills are learnable and available to us in an astonishing array. All the skills I mentioned in the consensus section are applicable here as well, and there are a few more to add.

Active and reflective listening is one key skill. When we have the intention to understand and to learn from each other, we listen differently. Curiosity helps with this (especially when we find ourselves starting to react to something someone is saying) and it is a skill that should be applied in equal measure to one's self and others. "Why am I feeling reactive?" is a more interesting and useful question than, "Why is so-and-so being such a jerk?," and yet the latter question is often where we go first. When we believe we're being attacked, invalidated, or unseen, it can be hard to turn our curiosity inward and seek first to understand ourselves.

It can be even harder to turn that curiosity outward: "What's behind what was just said? What's the speaker's story?" Doing that successfully can mean first making sure you heard it right (that's reflective listening) and then deepening your interest in the other person as a person with their own thoughts and feelings that are generating the words coming out of their mouth. This isn't conflict avoidance, but rather a healthier version of it: seeking understanding as a way to head off your own deeper reactivity.

What I just laid out is one version of addressing things early and often, and it helps head off a large amount of potentially tough conflict if you can practice it. "Early and often" is my mantra with clients trying to figure out how they lost their sense of community under layers of conflicted baggage that has built up over time. The first time you feel the reaction, name it and "curious" it to death. This helps immensely with conflicts that arise from misunderstandings and stylistic differences.

There are other kinds of conflict, too, mainly conflicts arising from genuine differences in needs, and conflicts arising from re-triggered old hurts.

Conflicts arising from differences in needs can be the hardest ones, and they are the territory of compromise and negotiation. The trick with those conflicts is to try to keep everyone out of taking anything personally: one person's need does not invalidate your need, but it may steer the group toward a solution or compromise that doesn't look perfect to anyone. This is the arena where we cede some personal territory to the group: in order to live with others, we don't get to construct our reality exactly as our cultural hyper-independence framework says we should be able to. It is worth seeing these moments as culture change in real time and space, and this is easiest when someone in the group can serve as an ally: not to the individuals involved but to the larger culture-change goals the group shares.

The final category is not the work of the group at all, but rather the work of individuals. When we find ourselves triggered into our old stuff, we need to both *do* something and *get* something. The doing is honesty: being able to self-reflect enough to see that this is our own stuff emerging and that it may or may not have anything to do with the situation we currently find ourselves in. This is especially hard because these triggering situations can be some of both: old stuff emerging that is making our emotions run higher than is needed, *and* some actually relevant stuff that the group will benefit from hearing. But it is hard to know that until the trigger is identified and managed as best we are able. So that is the *doing* part.

The *getting* is support. Just because someone is caught in the throes of an old trigger does not mean the group has permission to abandon them. We are here in part to provide absolutely needed social and emotional support for each other. Groups use a wide range of tools for this, and I don't have strong preferences around what you use, other than "whatever works" for your particular group. However, it is essential that the group has something in place in terms of known and accepted tools. Readily accessible tools that I trust and that multiple very functional communities have put to good use include:

- Nonviolent Communication
- Re-evaluation Co-counseling (also just called co-counseling)
- Restorative Circles.

Some conflicts either affect enough people, are disruptive enough to the full group functioning, or have elements in them that are tied closely to a community decision-making process, that a conflict crosses a line and becomes the group's business. When that happens, it is important to have clear agreements about what is expected of your members. Many groups use a sequence that looks something like this:

1. Attempt to work it out directly between you, using whatever method you can agree on. If that does not sufficiently resolves the conflict, then:

2. Work with a mediator who's been trained for that work and whom the community trusts, and that both of you feel good about. If that doesn't work, then:

3. Bring the conflict either to an official conflict resolution body for deeper help, or to the full group if it seems to warrant that level of attention.

Oftentimes, simply knowing there is this deep of a support system in place makes things a lot easier to resolve. I strongly recommend having some kind of a committee or team in place (and that goes for nonprofits and other social change groups, not just intentional communities) that can provide training for the community at large in conflict management, deeper training for mediators and facilitators, and in-the-moment calm and compassionate support should things progress to step 3.

There are more concrete tools and exercises for conflict management in *The Cooperative Culture Handbook*.

What Kind of Community?

So far, I have been talking about the things that all communities share in common. It doesn't matter if you are forming a cohousing community in a city or an ashram in the outback: you need to think about a lot of the same things in order to get it off the ground successfully. But of course, there are lots of important decisions in forming a community that will distinguish your group from all the other ones out there: besides location, these difference are the primary reason why new communities are formed. So this section is about the particular flavor of the community you want.

A Useful Tool for Founders and Seekers: Spectrums

I'm a little obsessed with spectrums. The world is pretty much one big grey area as near as I can tell. Anyone who has ever spent any time with me as a facilitator or a facilitation teacher knows that spectrums are one of my go-to tools.

In workshops I teach about starting an intentional community as well as finding a community home, I use this particular set of spectrums (see box on next page). These are things that every community lands on somewhere, either deliberately or by default.

Here's how I suggest people use them:

For Founders

It is very important that you get clear about what things are essential to you in your community vision and what things you don't really care about. I recommend going through these spectrums and marking on each one the perfect spot in your mind of how your community will be set up. (I do this with an X or some other simple symbol.) Then I would also mark (perhaps using a highlighter marker or brackets) your range of tolerance. In other words, you might have a preference, but for most of these you also will likely have some flexibility about how close to the ideal it needs to be in order for you to feel excited about all the work of creating a community.

As an example, you might ideally want to be very rural, but could live with being in a small town. So in that case, you'd mark an X all the way over on the far side above rural, and then place a bracket or highlighter mark from the rural side to, say, one-third of the way across the spectrum.

You may find that you have no opinion or preference for some of them. That's great! That means that your vision has some flexibility and will allow other people's preferences to come into play. However, it is very important to be as honest as you can be about your answers. If you really want to live in a community that is income sharing or has a strong spiritual orientation, it is fine to place an X and then have no brackets at all. This will help people who are considering joining you know exactly what they are joining.

Many founders make the mistake of thinking that they can answer all these questions after they have five or six or 10 people they really like who have decided to join. The pitfall in waiting to get clear about that is that you

---

Spectrums for Intentional Communities

ICs come in lots of flavors. Every group falls somewhere on these spectrums, which affect the feel, culture, and experience of being in the group (though be aware that the answers to these can change over time, and changes are not necessarily about how healthy or vibrant the group is). Misalignment in any one of these spectrums makes it a tough fit.

Income Sharing <———————————— Tithing ——————————> Independent Finances

High Resource Sharing <————————————————————————> Low Resource Sharing

No Cost to Join <————————————————————————————> High Cost to Join

Spiritually <——— Spiritually <——— Supports ———> Tolerates ———> Secular ———> Intolerant of
Same   Diverse   Spiritual Practice   Spirituality   Spirituality

Rural <————————————————————————————————————> Urban

Mission Driven <————————————————————> Member Quality of Life Driven

Inwardly Focused <————————————————————————> Outwardly Focused

Family Size <————————————————————————————> Village Size

Low Technology Use <————————————————————> High Technology Use

Mainstream Appeal <————————————————————————> Radical Appeal

Deep Alignment <——— Consensus <——— Voting ———> Small Decision Group ———> Sole Leader

Flat Power <——— Dispersed Power ———> Strong Pockets of Power ———> Very Lopsided

Strong Group Role   Group Hands Off
in Conflict Resolution <————————————————————> with Conflict Resolution

Rules-based <————————————————————————————> Relationally-based

"Moving Toward" Energy <————————————————————> "Resisting" Energy

run the risk of not having enough alignment among that group and wasting a lot of everyone's time.

Get clear about your must-haves, articulate those clearly, and recruit from that place. Then drag this spectrum worksheet out and let folks know that the group is welcome to answer the rest of those questions or just let yourselves default to something. Doing this well will create a much stronger, aligned, and clear core group to build from.

For People Seeking a Community

I recommend following the same procedure as above for seekers: mark on each of these spectrums your ideal and your range of tolerance. Then step back and do a little soul searching. You may have a preference, but how strong is it? Which ones of these are your make or break criteria? The same advice about honesty applies here. Be as real with yourself about these answers as you can be.

Hint: If each of your answers is just an X or has a very narrow range to it, you are likely to be very disappointed when you get out there and start searching. One of the first lessons of community is to be able to articulate your preferences and then widen back into flexibility for the sake of being able to connect and work with others. Filling this worksheet out is a first chance at seeing just how flexible or rigid you currently are. Having a strong preference on four to six of these is probably healthy and will help your search be productive.

Seekers should take this with them when they visit places. I'd recommend sitting down with someone who has been in the community you are visiting for a while (at least three years if the group is established) and asking them for their realistic take on their community and how well it matches your preferences. This can be an invaluable guide for sorting out the communities that might really work well for you.

Once you've narrowed your search in this more logical way, I'd recommend setting this aside and considering communities from a more intuitive or felt place. Regardless of what the spectrums say, which one feels right or the most like home? Is there a community that didn't quite match your answers, but your attention keeps getting drawn back to it? Can you flex and grow into that community? Is there something the spectrums didn't cover that you have found through your process really is more important than these criteria?

By the same token, if a place looks great on paper but feels wrong, trust your gut. Preferences can (and very likely will) change, but a good intuitive hit is almost always worth listening to.

Choosing an intentional community home is really all about being intentional. And generally, that will be a healthy mix of logic and love, criteria and intuition.

Nitty Gritty Stuff Ya Just Gotta Do

In order to create a solid foundation to operate from, communities need to deal with a number of things that, frankly, most of us detest. If you are one of those remarkable individuals who actually likes this stuff, I hereby anoint you a rare and wondrous commodity and hope your community appreciates you!

Category #1 is **getting your legal ducks in a row**. There's a lot to decide in terms of how you are going to be organized, and the legal structure is one of the core ones. I fully own that this is not my area of expertise: I'm including this because it is essential, not because I know a lot. The best current write-up that I've seen that you can use as an orientation guide to legal structures is a long article in the latest *Communities Directory*,[76] published by the Fellowship for Intentional Community (a slightly abridged version appears in *Communities* issue #173). In it, multiple long-time community advocates detail various choice points around the legal aspects and provide basic information to help your group make good decisions. The Directory is a valuable resource for a host of reasons, and when you are at the point of thinking about legal structures, this article alone will be worth the price of the book.

Before you get too deeply into investigating the legal structures, a core set of questions you will need to answer relate to ownership. Who owns the property, common structures, and homes will be a main determining factor for what legal structure(s) might suit your group best. If you already have a vision figured out, take your cues from that: what ownership structure will best empower that vision? How do you see people interacting with each other in the community, and how might your legal relationships affect that?

These questions get into some pretty deep philosophical territory, and can serve to further clarify how well aligned people are in your founding group. Major disagreements can surface here, and it is best to get these figured out prior to making any major financial commitments to each other. You can lose some folks at this stage, and that is probably better than getting in too much deeper before you really declare yourselves a community family.

Similarly, you have to dig into the second category: **financial relationships**. We tend to be pretty uncomfortable talking about money, but you just gotta do it. Basic questions include:

- Will you be income sharing or have independent finances?

- What financial obligations come with membership? Is there a buy-in fee (and if so, how will you use that money)? Are there monthly or yearly fees (and if so, what does a member get in return)?

- When someone leaves the community, are there financial exchanges that will happen at that point?

---

[76] *Communities Directory*, 7th edition, 2016, pp. 576–586. "Legal Structures for Intentional Communities in the US," by Diana Leafe Christian, Dave Henson, Albert Bates, and Allen Butcher. Diana deserves extra credit for doing the bulk of the work on this revision of a long-standing useful resource. The same article, minus some lesser-used legal structures and with some additional editing, appears on pages 46–55 of *Communities'* Winter 2016 issue.

- If you have independent finances, can people build equity while living in the community?

- Can people's heirs inherit property within the community? If so, are there caveats or processes around that which are different from any usual inheritance?

- Can people substitute labor contributions for fees that are normally expected to be paid with dollars?

- Will you have shared community businesses? Will you allow private businesses owned by members to operate from the property?

- What obligations is the community willing to take on in terms of aging in place or health-related crisis?

- If the community is income sharing, do you also share assets? How about debts?

Each of the above questions will likely sprout sub-questions as you get into talking about them. You want to make sure you are balancing clear expectations with being flexible enough to roll with reality and changes, as you are working on answering these; at least take those two poles into account. Some groups adopt fairly rigid systems and know that they will lose people as time goes on in part because of that rigidity. Just do it with your eyes open.

You will also need to balance protecting the group's rights and viability with protecting individuals' rights and viability. This will show up in both of the previous two categories, legal and financial arrangements, and can be especially challenging when property rights and equity building are up for conversation. It will also likely be a theme in the conversations I talk about in the next section: Seven Things Intentional Communities Always Fight About.

Remember that we are coming from a hyper-independent culture, and wanting to move toward something more cooperative. Keeping that in mind can help you do three important things:

1. Have compassion for people who find it hard to give up their personal right to do something: remember that they probably have no idea what anything else feels like and that this is safe territory. Because our sense of security is often tied to independence, core issues can get triggered in these conversations, and it is best to try to understand what someone's fears and concerns are about before forging ahead with a decision.

2. Craft policies with healthy interdependence as a guide, because that is where we want to get to. Policies that allow people to make this transition gradually can be good—this sometimes looks like having less-communal options for people when they are in a provisional membership. Having those six to 12 months of getting used to the idea of more cooperation and interdependence, while being able to witness other people doing it and reaping the benefits, is a kind thing to offer people.

3. Recognize that some people simply aren't going to be ready for that transition: it isn't their fault, but it might be a good indication that they aren't in the right group if the rest of you are ready to take that leap of faith and they can't quite do it.

The third sticky category is **developing entrance and exit processes**. I've already talked about the entrance part of this (above, in Membership Process). Exit from the community can take two forms: voluntary and involuntary. Unsurprisingly, voluntary is a lot easier.

The voluntary end to membership can come for a lot of reasons, and it's important for the community to understand what those reasons are. Someone may leave for reasons that have nothing to do with the community: a sick parent or new job requires relocation, the member is getting married to someone who isn't interested in community, the member is just ready for something new. While this can be sad, there isn't really anything for the community to do or respond to. In this case, the person's exit will be largely logistical and perhaps ceremonial (depending on the culture of the group). There should be a formal date when the person's membership ends, and all rights and responsibilities that come with membership should also end at that point. Just be clear when that is and what logistical (including any legal) things need to happen.

If a member is leaving and the reasons are about the community, then an added layer of process should ideally happen. If the member is willing, ask for written feedback or have someone they trust do an exit interview with them. Hopefully, the reasons have been thoroughly explored and there won't be any surprises, but sometimes new information emerges in this process. If it does, it is important for the community to do their best to take in the feedback and see if it points to problems the group wants to try to address. (Note: just because someone is angry or disappointed does not necessarily mean that the group is doing anything wrong. However, it behooves you to consider their feedback, regardless of how it is presented. Sometimes that anger contains important information that can help get the group back on track. It is best approached with curiosity.)

Involuntary loss of membership is a different animal. This is a situation where many in the group have come to a place of feeling that something is really not working with another person in the group, and the dynamic is significantly disruptive to the group function in some way. Often, a major cultural mismatch has emerged that wasn't apparent early on. Sometimes, there is abuse of some kind (or accusations thereof) or violation of group agreements. Always, there is pain.

Nobody wants to think about this at the beginning of the community-building process. A: it's a bummer. B: we are in the mode of building and seeking togetherness and acceptance and the last thing we want to think about is what to do if that doesn't pan out. C: most of us have some degree of conflict avoidance in us, and this situation represents a pretty tough conflict. And D: progressives (who constitute most of the likely readership of this book, as well as much of the intentional communities movement) often fancy ourselves able to accept anything and anyone, and bringing this up means we don't.

Nonetheless, nearly every group faces the need to ask a member to leave at some point. And it is far, far easier to manage if you have thought about the process that you will follow when there *isn't* a real human sitting in front of you driving you and much of the rest of the group to distraction. You are also much more likely to have a fair process if it is created during an un-triggered time. Waiting until you are up to your necks with someone and ready to kick them out almost guarantees bad process.

I want to focus mostly on what good process looks like, but first let me say that if the situation involves immediate danger of some sort, I strongly recommend not dealing with that without the back-up of local law enforcement. There can definitely be reasons to not do that, and you know your local law enforcement better than I do, but assuming they are basically solid folks who do their jobs well, and there really is a threat, please avail yourselves of their support. Not doing so can result in real tragedies sometimes.

That said, here's what I think good process looks like for the more common non-emergency situations:

- **Do your due diligence.** Use your conflict resolution process. Give the person a chance to change their behavior, and make and keep agreements. Just because someone bugs you doesn't mean they deserve to be kicked out. Focus on behavior, including responsiveness (or lack of it) to feedback. Make sure there are third parties involved, both to help it go as well as possible, and also to witness anything that is really egregious. Recognize that kicking someone out of their home is a very big deal and try to be understanding and patient with the person as those murmurs start to happen in the community.

- **Clear process, including the ability to protest.** At some point, when all of the above has failed, the continued unworkable behavior will trigger the start of a formal, full group process. There should be clear notification to the whole group that this process has started, and the process itself should include clear steps and timelines for how things progress to whatever the next step is. It is important that either the full group is aware of and has the option of participating in the proceedings, or the full group is aware of and has clearly ceded their authority for expulsion to a carefully chosen, even-handed body. Recognize that not everyone will be equally ready to give someone the boot, and expulsion involves loss of friendship for at least some people who will still be around when all is said and done.

  It's important to include in your process the person's right to protest and make their case for why they should be able to stay. This is not an organized and community-sanctioned witch-hunt. It should be a process that is deliberative and provides opportunity for all sides of the issue to be aired. That doesn't mean anyone has to agree with the person and/or their allies—simply that they have the right to be heard as well and to be able to respond to whatever frustrations and concerns people have with them. You also need a clear and clean end point. If that is a vote of X% of members, then that's what it is. If it is based on the recommendation of the conflict resolution team and ratified by your Board, then that's what it is. But make sure whatever process you design has a clear and knowable end point and that all your documents are in alignment on what that is.

- **Protecting Yourselves.** Build the possibility of expulsion into your by-laws and other core documents, including a membership agreement people sign (and possibly re-sign every few years). Most of the processes that I've witnessed or been a part of over the years have involved people who have a worldview that leans toward litigious, and a personality that is combative and stubborn, especially when feeling threatened. (There are more and less polite versions of this, but that package seems pretty standard.) Because litigious is on that list, you want to make sure you are being very diligent about documenting the steps you've taken, saving any emails that were part of the communication, and absolutely following your own process.

- **Healing.** Expelling someone sucks. There is almost no way for it to *not* suck. (If there is, I have certainly never seen it.) Make sure to build into the process recognition that people will have emotional processing that needs to happen along the way. And make time after the person leaves for coming back together as a community and supporting each other in the healing process.

  Healing is going to look different for different people. Looking honestly at how things got to the point of someone being expelled can be an important part of the process for some people, and will just feel petty and like having salt rubbed in the wound for others. Some people will want to gather as soon as the final decision is made, others will not be able to mourn it or vent about it or whatever they need to do until the person has actually left. So make sure you make space for different versions of what healing means. But don't skip this step. Some ongoing relationships have probably been strained, and working those through as best you can will help your community return to a feeling of wholeness and togetherness.

The Seven Things Intentional Communities Always Fight About

Certain issues always seem to arise in communities. My list (which could probably be added to by others long involved with the movement) are these:

cleaning, noise, pets, kids, work, money, and food.[77] All of these issues have a few things in common:

1. They are areas we are told by our culture are our "personal" business. What we eat, how we raise our kids, how we make and spend money… these are all touchy subjects that we generally avoid because they are "no one else's business." Except, when you get into community, the private/public lines get redrawn. If your dog digs up my flowers, your child is constantly screaming in public spaces, you don't clean up after yourself, or you can't pay your part of the community fees, the impact is much more direct than it is in a regular neighborhood. These issues become not only a source of conflict, but a source of cultural change because even talking about them was previously defined as taboo.

2. At the same time, they are, collectively, a large portion of what governments regulate. Think about local and state laws: we have schooling and child-treatment laws, most towns have a local pound to catch animals who aren't being cared for, we regulate food safety, pay people to clean our streets, support all of this with a tax base that we vote about changing at almost every election, call the cops on each other for being too loud at night, etc. Thus, these are issues at nearly every scale of cooperative endeavor: from what couples fight about (money and housework being top items on that list) to what major cities invest vast resources in trying to mitigate conflict and risk around. Thus:

3. These are nearly universal areas of conflict and policy-making. You will have to deal with them in the small circle of your community-building—that's just the reality.

So my recommendation is this: the first time you bump into these issues, consider yourselves to have progressed to the point of taboo-breaking realness in your group. I'm not going to say, "Celebrate it!" (because that kind of pollyanna approach to things has made me crazy since I first started doing community). As spiritually advanced as that may be, no one wants to throw a party when their community hits their first major conflict—for many, that is a major moment of questioning and soul searching, most frequently done in a more somber and contemplative mood.

I think of it, rather, as earning your "Welcome to the Human Race" card as a group. One of these issues is frequently the first real opportunity for groups to try their hand at conflict resolution and challenging policy-making. You may not pop the champagne, but you can recognize it for being a natural and needed part of maturing as a group, and not freak out.

---

[77] My mentor in facilitation and community process, Laird Schaub, has an amusing article with a more expansive list than mine, wherein the main conflict points all start with the letter "P." It is called "Minding Your P's for Cues" and appeared in *Communities* issue #143, Summer 2009.

My basic advice is this: don't panic or throw in the towel over one of these. I've seen groups who literally stop trying to do community at this point—they decide community can't work, or that the work isn't worth it. If you do give up based on one of these issues, you have just done three things: 1) passed the buck to your local officials who get to deal with this stuff whether they like it or not; 2) let an opportunity for cultural change that you very much want pass you by; and 3) given up on your own community dreams. And that is a losing proposition for everyone.

The Importance of Orientation

Orienting newcomers is incredibly important. Here are a few truisms related to that:

- Moving to community almost always brings with it a form of culture shock that very few people anticipate in their excitement to move in.

- Founders and other long-term members often don't understand the newcomers' perspective because, having designed the community or lived there forever, it all seems pretty intuitive to them.

- There's a ton of context and unspoken stuff in a well-established community.

- People learn in different ways, and one kind of orientation isn't going to cut it.

- The power gap between old and new members is real, and will get bigger and more problematic the worse the group is at orientation.

Leadership and Power in Community

One of the most important paradigms that I have studied in the last 10 years is spiral dynamics integral, a cultural evolution system initially articulated by anthropologist Claire Graves in the 1950s and built on significantly by Ken Wilber in more recent years.[78] One of the very provocative aspects of this is understanding how our relationship to hierarchy differs greatly within different worldviews, and evolves naturally as those worldviews evolve. The system uses colors as shorthand for the evolutionary stages it describes, and I'll use them here too.

At the Blue stage, hierarchy is seen as an unquestioned good, a natural state of things based on morally-infused, righteous power. That power derives in part from religious authority, and in part from a kind of "might makes right" approach to life. Morality is pretty black and white here. In this worldview, if you are at the bottom of the hierarchy, you likely deserve that because of some moral failing.

---

[78] The best easy-to-follow explanation of spiral dynamics integral is in Ken Wilber's *A Theory of Everything: An Integral Vision for Business, Politics, Science, and Spirituality* (Shambala Press, 2000).

At the next stage, Orange, hierarchy is based on a meritocracy: if you are good at something, you'll rise in the ranks, and your position is due to skill and your ability to effectively compete with others. This is climbing the corporate ladder. This worldview also birthed affirmative action out of the idea that everyone deserves an equal ability to compete for society's goods.

The Green stage comes next, and one of its core beliefs is a pretty strong rejection of hierarchy: it sees the only good society being an egalitarian one where everyone's voices are heard and valued. Any ranking at all is resisted: no ideas are better than any other, nor any people. In this worldview, if you are disempowered, it is likely the system's fault. This stage births justice movements: people have the right to full dignity and respect regardless of what you think of them morally, and regardless of what they contribute to the economy.

All of these three stages I've just mentioned have one characteristic in common: they think the other worldviews are flat-out wrong, or even dangerous. That distinguishes them from the next stage, Yellow, which is a kind of integrative one.

This stage looks at the early ones and sees both folly and merit in each. Having a strong moral framework that allows you to discern right from wrong is beneficial, as is meritocracy. Oppression is a real phenomenon, listening to all voices is great, and systems analysis incredibly valuable. So this last stage that I'm going to talk about is one that is more about functionality and finding what really works, without all the judgment. In some ways, it is more about practicality than dogma, and sees people with a wide range of worldviews as potentially being part of the broader "family" or "tribe," and worthy of being listened to.

In this stage, hierarchy is neither good nor bad: it's a tool. How someone (or a group of people) relates to hierarchy is a reliable indicator of what their theory of power and leadership is. Power can be derived from moral authority, from being a good competitor, or from a group sense. In reality, it is derived from all of those things, and that makes power a messy topic. It is also messy because how it is used and misused is viewed very differently by different people. And what defines good leadership is also closely tied in with where power comes from, and on whose behalf you ought to be using it.

Most secular intentional communities are solidly Green in their orientation to hierarchy, leadership, and power: the ultimate authority is the group itself and everyone should have a strong voice in determining what that group will is. It is why consensus is such a popular decision-making method in communities: it meshes much better with Green than any other way of making decisions does. (Sole leader systems, or ones with a strong hierarchy that leads to a single figure, are appealing to Blue, and the competitive vibe of voting appeals most to Orange.) Green has at its heart a very deep care and compassion, both of which are necessary to have a real sense of community.

There are, however, downsides to Green. Chief among them are 1) the length of time it takes to have everyone feel safe, heard, and valued, and then to come up with a solution that works for all, 2) a kind of counter-intuitive narcissism that can flourish in such a thoroughly group-oriented system: if my feelings are really important, then that can reinforce my belief that they should take priority over everything else, and the group seems to allow this, and 3) the inability to clearly discern the best decision because of the resistance to passing judgment on anyone or any ideas. Green can be, in fact, highly suspicious of any wielding of power at all, seeing in it Blue moralism and lack of interest in the plight of those with less power, or Orange hyper-competitiveness and ladder-climbing. This resistance can be incredibly frustrating for people who are simply trying to get something done.

The disadvantages are, in fact, why people who have been solidly Green for a good amount of time can start itching in their skins to do something different. They encourage people to move on to that next stage of Yellow, where they start seeing with new eyes some of the things they previously felt a lot of judgment about, and wondering if they may, after all, have something valuable to offer a functional group. Thus, Yellow is born.

My experience with Yellow is that there is a strong draw toward what I call "hierarchy lite." Delegation of not only responsibility but authority to decide and act in a particular area is an example of this. While the power to do so comes from the group originally, the group cedes a certain amount of that power to a single person or committee that is carefully selected, based on some combination of trustworthiness, skill, and experience. This is a form of meritocracy, but not one granted because someone outcompeted everyone else. It is more about someone's ability to serve the mission of the group.

And that's the core of Yellow: it is mission-oriented. That makes it a really good match for *intentional* communities: it is all about what is going to support the intention behind our coming together, and while it isn't interested in running roughshod over an individual's feelings or desires, it also isn't going to sacrifice the group's viability to them. What Yellow serves is *intention* more than *personalities*.

So enough for theory: what does this translate into concretely for communities? The previous section on decision-making describes what I think functional consensus process looks like, and some of those recommendations are very much in alignment with a Yellow worldview: making sure you validate blocks, relying on delegation to get a chunk of the work done, and making sure people understand the difference between being heard and being agreed with.

I also think it means having a strong willingness as a group to talk about power, rather than to not talk about it. Groups steeped too deeply in Green can have a very hard time acknowledging that power differences exist in their groups, and what you can't acknowledge, you can't talk about. My take on power is that it is necessary to get anything done. And that's different than saying it is a necessary evil: power is a necessary good. Action requires power, as does effectiveness. The holding of power can lead to blind spots on the part of the wielder of it, and the use of it can lead to people getting hurt (sometimes badly) by its careless use. Given that so many of us have past damage around power (very real trauma that feeds into the Green suspicion of it) it's hard not to make mistakes with it. I'd say that that's OK—but what isn't OK is not talking about it. When it comes to social behaviors, we only really learn through dialogue and feedback.

Related to all of this, I strongly recommend that groups have a conversation about what they want in their leaders, and develop a community philosophy of leadership. Some people are likely to have more of a Blue paradigm, some more of an Orange one, and others, a Green one. Without having a deliberate exploration and coming to a shared understanding of this, there will likely be a confused (and contradictory) hodge-podge of ideas and expectations laid on people who try to step up and get things done. And that's messy. Failing to be clear about this area, and instead getting mad at each other when it doesn't go well, is likely to lead to people avoiding leadership responsibilities in your community: who wants to be the target of anger based on unclear expectations and mixed messages?

The Cooperative Culture Handbook includes a number of exercises and conversation prompts around power and leadership if you are seeking further guidance on these topics.

Creating Regionally Connected Networks

Self-sufficiency is romantic as hell. I remember backpacking regularly in my early 20s; there was nothing quite like knowing that everything I needed was on my back. There is a freedom, a cleanness, to that that is incredibly liberating in an age when we are practically drowning under the weight of the stuff we own.

I got a more mature taste of this when I lived in a couple different communities that grew a lot of their own food...and then again living off-grid. Each time, there was a glorious low-level euphoria that I experienced, thinking that if something bad happened, I would be one of the people still eating.

Euphoria aside, every one of those experiences was a bit of a lie. The backpacking trip would end after a couple weeks, that food was grown using imported manure from someone else's farm and seeds from a catalog, and those solar panels were hardly made by my own two hands. We love the thought of self-sufficiency: it appeals to our American pride in independence. But actually achieving it is another matter.

And frankly, I'm not sure it is desired. You know Waco, Texas? One of the more notorious intentional communities of the last century, David Koresh's Branch Davidians, put Waco on the map. The problem is, they took it too far—cutting themselves off from their neighbors, turning whatever was really happening inside the walls of their compound into a gloriously frightening mystery for the people around them. Details aside (and some of them are genuinely messed up, no matter how you look at it) part of why the situation went from spectacularly uncomfortable for the neighbors to an FBI-initiated bloodbath was an extreme manifestation of the self-sufficiency urge: if we can hole ourselves up within these walls in some survivalist fantasy, everything will be OK.

I use the Branch Davidians as an example of what *not* to do as a community: don't cut yourself off from the neighbors. (And especially don't do it while visibly stockpiling guns, but that's a conversation for another time.) You need *allies* as a community. It isn't unusual for someone "in town" to take a disliking to or to mistrust the "different" thing happening just down the road. If you regularly socialize with and do exchange with other people in townw, and you are basically decent people, the rumors will get quelled by your allies, or at least they will have your back if things get tense.

This is essential for many communities' long term viability.

The other reason to not try too hard to be self-sufficient is that it takes a lot of pressure off the community. If you are part of the region, both contributing and engaging in exchange, you will be a valued part of that wide community. You will have access to a wider range of services, skills, products, and most importantly foods, than you are going to be able to create and grow on your own.

The scale a community needs to operate at in order to be truly self-sufficient is probably in the thousands of members—in other words, a small town or neighborhood. Being totally self-sufficient at a smaller scale is possible, if you pare your needs down to the absolute bare essentials (nothing manufactured, everything from materials and crops that come from your land itself—like Little House on the Prairie, minus the traveling peddlers, or the tools the Wilder family brought with them). It might be fun to try at summer camp, but it is a life of deprivation when that simply isn't necessary.

So you will be "importing" things into your community. Striving to be as self-sufficient as is reasonable is a fine goal, and one that will push your community to greater creativity. And the closer you get, the more insulated you will be if things go badly awry. One of the things I like about that is that it puts you in a position to be in service to others in crisis—if you have the skills, the seeds, the hand tools, and the mindset that has developed over the years that you can feed yourself, you are going to be in demand when others suddenly find they need these things. If yours is the one house with electricity and water that still runs, you can help out other people when the city utilities suddenly go down.

At the same time, past a certain point, pushing yourself too hard to do the incredibly difficult might actually have downsides significant enough as to be not worth it. We really need something more akin to regional self-sufficiency, rather than individual or small community self-sufficiency. If we could get most of our needs met within 100 miles of home and nearly all of them within 500 miles of home, that would be pretty impressive (and would represent incredible reductions in carbon emissions damage).

It would also bring us into deep, and much more personal relationship with the people who occupy our region. That's a practice of interdependence that puts us back in touch with something much more like how the natural world operates. The principles can be the same, even if the actual manifestation includes tractors and cell phones. And don't forget that interdependence is the sweet spot in our cooperative culture model.

The Ability to Re-Vision

A lot of this chapter has been about starting an intentional community. This final part is about how to keep your community going once you are landed and living together. I've already touched on good decision-making and conflict resolution, and those are the most critical elements for longevity. Beyond those, the most critical skill is being able to shift gears when that is called for. Some groups get locked into their original vision so strongly that it is almost as if the members would rather see it die than engage in reasonable revision. And that's a mistake.

I've had several community clients who were between 15 and 20 years old and who had found themselves kind of itching in their collective skin. The old vision had some serious dust on it, their conflicts had become entrenched, and newer (often younger, but not necessarily) people had come in with different ideas about how the vision could be manifested or brought up to date. This age range for communities often seems to bring with it a strong need to hit the reset button.

A lot changes in a couple decades, and I think this is a healthy urge that keeps communities not only alive but vibrant into the mature phase of community.

So what might that look like? For many of the groups I work with, this is a literal re-visioning. I detail what that process can look like in *The Cooperative Culture Handbook*, and encourage groups that are at that stage to utilize that resource. Some groups do a good job of evolving steadily, and nothing dramatic is needed, even in this window where you are going from a young to a mature community. This tendency to constantly evolve adds a vibrancy and aliveness to a community, and these are some of the best places to live. For some groups, this shift might come in the form of a number of old policies, even core ones, coming up for revision. This happened at Dancing Rabbit while I was there.

In 2013, Dancing Rabbit made a major decision: to go from being entirely off the electrical grid to hooking up and becoming a net exporter of electricity.

Over a year of careful deliberation went into this decision. People were concerned that the community would be less conservation-minded without black-out days to remind us of our limits. Others didn't like the inherent eco-ugliness that is the grid structure. And still others had financial concerns about investing in such a big piece of infrastructure. Turns out that all of these concerns had some legitimacy, and the decision led to the usual mix of unintended and unhoped-for consequences.

And yet it showed some real flexibility and creativity on the part of the community. While we gave up the easy-to-understand label of "off-grid community" (which has a flavor of seriousness to it that most people understand immediately) what we gained was three-fold: 1) it is both easier and a bit more financially accessible to build a house now in the community; 2) DR now models a non-insular expression of ecological values—the neighbors just down the road now use some % of green energy as well, and the community's impact now tangibly extends beyond their borders; and 3) the community was able to have one less fossil-fuel powered car, replacing one of the old cars with a Leaf.

This is one really good example of a group deepening into its stated values over time by exercising their flexibility and deliberative skills. Most successful communities embody some element of this flexibility through time.

Another example comes from Twin Oaks. The book the community took its initial modeling from included a system of childcare that essentially disconnected caregiving from reproducing: kids were cared for by people who were excited about taking care of kids, and that didn't necessarily include their biological parents. A kids' building was built that was kid-scale, and all the kids lived in that building, with their caregivers also having rooms there.

On the scale of Twin Oaks' history, the experiment was fairly short-lived. Turns out that at least some of the kids really wanted a real connection to their parents, and not all the parents were thrilled about the experiment either. So, in spite of this being an important part of Twin Oaks' early identity as a community, they changed. While a lot of non-parents are still involved with childcare, children there now have a much more traditionally family-centered upbringing.

Regardless of whether the community does a full reboot, gradual evolution, or piecemeal deep revisions, the willingness to look with fresh eyes at our communities is a core skill for longevity. The work of asking, "who are we and why are we doing this?" doesn't end once the community is established. And with climate disruption starting to rear its ugly head, I expect a lot of groups to be thrust into asking those questions sooner and more frequently. The next chapter looks at what some of that work might entail.

Chapter 5: Everyone's Work:
Culture and Emotional Integration

Regardless of whether you live in a community or have opted to stay an independent operator, there is work that we can all do to transform our culture and ourselves with the goal of being better able to rationally deal with climate disruption. This is true whether we have already passed the point of no return and a climate apocalypse is inevitable or if we still think we have time to pull out a collective win for humanity and avoid collapse.

I consider these things to be "everyone's work" because mainstream culture kinda sucks for most of us in some significant ways. Social isolation, economic insecurity, and rising health crises related to environmental degradation (to name a few fairly universal experiences among Americans attempting to go it alone) are all simple facts of life for far too many people. Remedies to all of these exist, and they require both cultural transformation and parallel significant personal worldview shifts.[79]

Worldview: The Heart of the Matter

Our worldview is the fundamental lens (or set of lenses) that we see the world through. Like the infamous rose-colored glasses, our worldview colors everything we see, and it is the foundational set of beliefs that drive all of our decision-making. Everyone has a worldview. It might be secular or spiritual, cynical or optimistic, hierarchical or egalitarian, self-protective or open, but rest assured, you and everyone around you have some package of baseline beliefs that drive everything you do.

Another way to see worldview is that it is the foundation to your house. Everything is built on top of it. Coherent lives are built on top of coherent

---

[79] Please note that the inclusion of worldview shifts should not in any way be interpreted as victim-blaming. The reason people's lives suck and don't work is not that they aren't thinking the right way. I think these problems are rooted in deep-seated cultural beliefs expressed in systems that are far bigger than anyone's personal consciousness can overcome. I have them paired together because changing our culture will also require shifts in our personal worlds: I'm attempting to introduce a different system in this book that people can choose to embrace if they want to. That shift will change you if you do it. *In other words, I put the causative onus on the system, not on individuals.*

worldviews. Contradictory lives are built on top of contradictory worldviews. Cognitive dissonance (when a new piece of information comes into play that disrupts your worldview) can temporarily result in seemingly contradictory decisions. In the modern world, where we are exposed to so many different ideas and ways of looking at things, it can be hard to ever feel fully settled. This is both exhilarating and disconcerting. (The more rigid our worldview was in the first place, the more likely it is to lean toward disconcerting. Either that or you get very good at actively blocking out any new information, no matter how valuable it might be for you to take it in instead.)

Without examination and self-reflection, we generally default to the worldview of the mainstream culture around us and our family of origin's take on it. This is one way that cultures are fundamentally conservative and stable things. It is also why social change is often experienced as disruptive and teenagers are often experienced as rebellious: questioning is antithetical to the culture or family system maintaining its momentum.

Cultures also have their own trajectories. You can think of a culture as being a very, very large ship, slowly moving in some direction. And you can think of each one of us being a rower for that huge ship. When we pull in the same direction as everyone else, we are contributing to that direction. When we pull in a different direction, we minutely affect the direction of the whole boat. (Plus, metaphorically speaking, our arms get really tired. Ask any long-time activist who has worked on change for an extended period of time. That shit's exhausting.) Thus, our individual worldview has a small influence on the collective worldview.

Social movements that are effective understand this and aim to influence as many people as possible to see something differently than the way the wider culture is seeing it, and appeal to people's values to motivate change. This is part of why Joanna Macy's model of understanding successful movements includes the element of worldview changes. This is also part of why storytelling is becoming a more prominent part of a lot of activist trainings: a compelling story changes how we view the world.

Worldview change is an iterative process. We change how we see something, and that changes our decisions. Once we implement those decisions, our life changes, which causes shifts in how we see things. Any problem or situation looked at from a different angle will look different, and when you change something in your life, you are placing yourself at a different angle of viewing.

There are three key places for us to do worldview work at this time, which relate directly to climate disruption:

1. Define and move toward the culture we want.

2. Deal with our racism, sexism, and classism.

3. Do our emotional work related to fears, anxiety, mourning, and anger about climate disruption.

Let's take them one at a time.

The Culture We Want

George Monbiot recently published an essay[80] that does an excellent job of summing this up. He writes:

> [H]uman beings, the ultrasocial mammals, whose brains are wired to respond to other people, are being peeled apart. Economic and technological change play a major role, but so does ideology. Though our wellbeing is inextricably linked to the lives of others, everywhere we are told that we will prosper through competitive self-interest and extreme individualism. ...
>
> Consumerism fills the social void. But far from curing the disease of isolation, it intensifies social comparison to the point at which, having consumed all else, we start to prey upon ourselves.
>
> This does not require a policy response.[81] It requires something much bigger: the reappraisal of an entire worldview. Of all the fantasies human beings entertain, the idea that we can go it alone is the most absurd and perhaps the most dangerous. We stand together or we fall apart.

So we need each other, and we aren't going to get an adequate amount of community if we just go along for the ride with the western society default.

It helps to understand more deeply what we are talking about when we speak about culture. It is like water to fish: it can be very difficult to actually see what we are swimming in. Fortunately a lot of research has been done that can take apart this complex thing called culture and highlight different aspects of it. I find these models to be very helpful in understanding what our challenges are (and also understanding how we have gotten ourselves into this mess of climate disruption, simply by not swimming upstream). So let's look more closely at a particular aspect of culture.

Let's start simple:

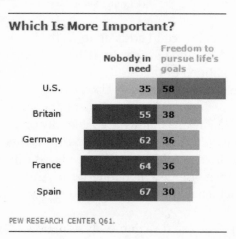

Which Is More Important?

	Nobody in need	Freedom to pursue life's goals
U.S.	35	58
Britain	55	38
Germany	62	36
France	64	36
Spain	67	30

PEW RESEARCH CENTER Q61.

---

[80] Read the full article at *The Guardian*'s blog, www.theguardian.com/commentisfree/2016/oct/12/neoliberalism-creating-loneliness-wrenching-society-apart.

[81] I'll make the case in Chapter 6 for why I don't think policy and culture are easily separable, and that's my only disagreement with Monbiot's article.

This first chart shows our general orientation toward taking care of each other, versus focus on personal achievement. In contrast to other western nations with a similar level of development, we lean strongly toward the individual end of the spectrum on this one, rather than the communal care end.

This next chart looks at the United States through six different lenses, called the Hofstede's indices. (Note that the numbers on the chart refer to the index for each area, and there were a number of factors the researchers took into account for each item.) As you can see, the US is strongly individualistic—in fact, we are the most individualistic country in the world, according to this study.[82]

United States

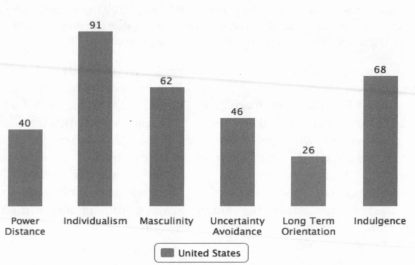

To summarize what this chart adds up to: in the US we tend to be relatively tolerant of power differentials in groups (that's Power Distance). Most people in "developed" nations in this study were less tolerant than Americans. We are highly individualistic, and are also strongly masculine (meaning, in this system, that we are driven by achievement and competition). Our uncertainty avoidance rating means that we are generally one of the countries more comfortable with the unknown—but that also means that we tend to take our chances with how things unfold and will not necessarily try to shape things. We are more short-term oriented than long-term. And finally, we have a high indulgence rating, which is pretty much exactly what it sounds like—we like our comforts.

In looking at this, you can do a fine analysis of how US culture was primed to do exactly what we've done in terms of climate policy. We've avoided

---

[82] Note: there is a more full exploration of American culture based on the Hofstede's measurements in Appendix I.

thinking about the long-term consequences, because we have a confidence in our ability to weather change, and because to look seriously at it would mean to not indulge ourselves. And we have used a very competitive and individualistic lens to see other countries through.

The Uncertainty Avoidance is especially interesting to me—it is likely a big contributing factor to the role we have played in climate change, because we are lackadaisical about future trouble: we'll deal with it when it comes, and aren't necessarily going to alter our behavior to head off change just because it is change. On the other hand, it means we might do better than most when changes suddenly confront us. Unfortunately, our behavior is going to drag a lot of other cultures that don't deal as well with change right along with us.

And, finally, the power differences between countries don't really bother us enough to make much impact on our policies—we just aren't wired culturally to take justice particularly seriously if it is inconvenient for us or reduces our ability to compete well. That may seem harsh, but I find this particular analysis to explain a lot: it's not as simple as selfishness, but rather has to do with how we relate to power in a fundamental way. This helps make my case that cultural change is imperative, because our behavior is creating disastrous effects for millions (and soon to be billions) of people around the world.

The following chart is one that I've been developing for the last five years, based on what I have seen in working with many intentional communities and nonprofits (both as a trainer and consultant and as a member of those groups). You can hear echoes of the Hofstede analysis of the US in the "Extreme Competitive" column.

Comparing Cultural Worldviews
and the behaviors that come from them

Extreme Competitive Culture	Sustainable Cooperative Culture	Extreme Cooperative Culture
Compete with others	Cooperate, including collaboration with allies	Cooperate within; collaborate only with others your group fully agrees with
Seek advantage and winning	Seek understanding and effective action	Seek attention as connection
Have skill? Use to dominate	Have skill? Teach with discernment	Have skill? Give away indiscriminately
Loudest voices win	Collaboration/consensus with discernment	Consensus with no discernment

Extreme Competitive Culture	Sustainable Cooperative Culture	Extreme Cooperative Culture
I-oriented (individualistic, focus on self)	We-oriented (communal, focus on self in balance with others)	Us-oriented (hyper-communal, self subsumed to group)
Independence encouraged/celebrated	Interdependence encouraged/celebrated	Codependence encouraged/celebrated
Dis-integrated	Integrated with differences valued	Individual needs/strengths lost
Capitalize on circumstances	Empathize with circumstances	Pity circumstances
Protect (resources and emotions, with no risk)	Share (resources and emotions, with boundaries)	Share (resources and emotions, without boundaries)
Make others responsible	Recognize personal and collective responsibility	Over-own personal responsibility
Differences threaten me	Differences are interesting	Differences threaten the group
Narcissism based on being "the best" and not needing to care	Not narcissistic: self is valued member of valued team	Narcissism based on emotional neediness met by group
Systems serve me	Service to others	Martyrdom

(Note: harking back to the last chapter's discussion of power and leadership and spiral dynamics, these columns roughly correlate to Orange with lingering bits of Blue on the left, an unhealthy embodiment of Green on the right, and Yellow in the center column.)

While I spend a lot of time unpacking this chart and offering exercises for exploration in *The Cooperative Culture Handbook*, I want to provide a brief discussion of it here as well. I believe it is critically important for us to understand that the climate problem is, as much as anything, a *cultural* problem. One key piece of this is that our culture has primed us to accept capitalism as a "natural" form of economics—it fits perfectly with the competitive, advantage-seeking, independent aspects of our mainstream culture. And that economic system is driving ecological destruction, even while the culture itself gives rise to mental illness and isolation.

So what are the alternatives? We need to be looking toward building a culture where resources are used to serve the interests of the whole, not only the most effective competitors. This means a restoration of the Commons as a fundamental principle, where we are collectively managing our resources from much more of an interdependent, empathetic, "we" orientation.

Sustainable cooperative culture aligns well with a form of socialism, but goes well beyond that, to be a system that integrates culture and an understanding that economics is not just about exchange. It asks us fundamental questions: who do we see as "our people"? How do we want to get our needs met? What happens when economics is a subset of ecology, rather than the other way around? Those are versions of these questions, writ large in the national political scene.

Community is a place where we come into direct personal (and interpersonal) contact with these kinds of fundamental questions: they wear the faces of our companions; they arise when we try to figure out how to get the work done; they insert themselves when we are all in this project together, but people of different means and physical ability have different pieces to bring to the table and it gets messy; and they come directly into the room when we try to set ecological goals and realize that conversation is limited by what we can "afford" — and "afford" has been defined for us by a system that makes our skin crawl.

Trying to either solve the climate crisis or build community on top of a competitive, independence-glorying culture simply doesn't work: there are too many deep internal contradictions. So these cultural questions are going to cause us a lot of soul-searching, and are going to drop us into cognitive dissonance on a regular basis. We can pursue stop-gap measures that buy us time (and indeed, I recommend some of those in Chapter 6, because they do move us incrementally toward something better) but the real changes that need to happen are much deeper than simply finding the best way to manage within our current culture.

The first step in those big underlying changes is understanding where we are headed, and that is the main reason I include the cultural worldviews chart in this book. It's the compass we need to set our direction by.

Race, Class, Gender, and Climate Change

Climate change is deeply intertwined with race, class, and gender. I'll talk more in the next chapter about the economics of climate change, but for now, I'd like to focus on the *who* of different roles we are all playing in the crisis.

First off, note what countries have historically contributed the largest amount to climate change. These are wealthy nations whose political systems are dominated by white people: the US, Canada, European countries, and Australia. The inventions of white people (the internal combustion engine most notably) and the high-consumption cultures and habits of the western, white world have landed us where we are today.

Certainly not everyone who lives in these countries is white, but note who controls the political dialogs and economic agendas in these places. Note as well that the resistance to the policies of heavy consumption of fossil fuels has come most strongly, the world over, from indigenous people, who are neither wealthy (in the ways we typically conceptualize wealth) nor powerful.

Now look from the other end—the impact our actions have had. The places in the world that have thus far taken the brunt of climate effects are largely poor, brown people: witness Syria, India, Thailand, the Maldive Islands, Brazil, China, and within the US, heavily Hispanic Florida, heavily black New Orleans, and Louisiana as a whole, one of the poorest states in the country.

Louisiana's lost land is particularly illustrative of climate dynamics. D. Phil Turnipseed, the director of the US Geological Service National Wetlands Research Center, calls Louisiana's shrinking profile "the worst environmental and socioeconomic disaster in North America." Approximately 1,900 square miles of land mass have disappeared from the familiar boot-shaped map of the state, according to the USGS.[83] When you look at the currently accurate map it is shocking—it's about one third of the state, gone. In those areas in Louisiana where the wealthy have been hit as strongly as the poor, the recovery efforts have been disproportionately going to the wealthier places and neighborhoods, according to the National Housing Institute.

In short, climate change is a problem largely created by (relatively) wealthy white people, and it is a crisis most strongly affecting (relatively) poor brown people.

Further, the people who have most consistently put their lives on the line to stop the fossil fuel industry are disproportionately people of color. One study discovered that, on average, one to two people die each week in a climate-related protest. And 60% of those people are indigenous.

From Al Jazeera:

> The murders of land and environmental defenders are on the rise. According to a recent report by London-based advocacy organization Global Witness, at least 116 environmentalists were killed last year. More than 75 percent of the deaths occurred in Central and South America. Most people died resisting oil and mineral extraction, land grabs by agribusiness, logging and other mega-development projects.[84]

The article goes on to highlight the case of one of the best-known indigenous activists killed in recent years, Berta Carceras in Honduras. Standing Rock may have been the biggest indigenous-led protest, but it was far from the first.

All of this means we need to see climate disruption in the context of human rights. Those rights include access to clean air and water, and a stable climate. They also push many of us to civil disobedience, and that results in a variety of additional human rights violations which are also disproportionately suffered by people of color and the poor.

---

[83] Information and quote from Brett Anderson in the Matter blog, Sept 8, 2014.

[84] Lauren Carasik. 2015. "Land Rights Defenders Face Growing Threats." america.aljazeera.com/opinions/2015/5/land-rights-defenders-face-growing-threat.html.

And many of the potential solutions to climate change are almost as bad from an economic justice standpoint. A flat-out carbon tax would be regressive and make it even harder for poor people to manage the most basic things such as getting to work and putting food on their family's tables.[85] The geoengineering solutions, when you look at them closely (if they worked at all) are most likely to make the global north safer, and deflect the worst disruptions onto the global south, reinforcing the systemic racism and classism that exist at a global level between countries.[86]

Switching over to small-scale organic agriculture is a terrific idea (and indeed a 2013 UN report makes a very strong case that small scale, organic agriculture is the best option to not only feed the world, but manage climate change). However, the way agriculture subsidies work in the US, organic agriculture isn't really helping the poor (unless they are fortunate enough to be able to grow it themselves, as in the urban agriculture examples in Chapter 2). One of the reasons Chapter 6 focuses so much on regulatory reform is that many of the best ideas for fixing the climate crisis are regressive within the current regulatory and subsidy frameworks.

Class-regressive policies also disproportionately impact women, especially single women who are parents. And climate change is already hitting women harder than men in many places. According to the UN, women are usually much harder hit by natural disasters and less able to access relief afterward.

In one particular UN study in China (where climate change has already hit harder than in most places in the world) women make up 70% of the agricultural workforce (which has already been seen to be an especially hard-hit population in other countries) and have less access to other work opportunities, land, technology, and loans which would make that easier to manage. They also have less knowledge of emergency plans than men. And that's just one example of how this growing crisis plays out along gender lines.

Bottom line is that we can't solve the climate crisis without simultaneously looking deeply at racism, sexism, and economic injustice. And that means work: hard work to root racism, sexism, and classism out of both our individual consciousnesses and our collective culture and systems.

Black Lives Matter has done an amazing job of bringing a lot more attention to race issues in the US, and doing it in a way that is unapologetic, clear, and invitational for others to join in. Activists like Van Jones have long been drawing attention to the links between race and the environment. We have a long way to go in following the lead of people of color, and for us white folks,

---

[85] An innovative version of the carbon tax comes from Citizens' Climate Lobby, who advocate for what they call "carbon fee and dividend." It would return all collected monies directly and equitably to the American people, helping to alleviate the regressive nature of the tax while getting the benefits of encouraging lower carbon consumption.

[86] This analysis is thoroughly laid out in Naomi Klein, *This Changes Everything*, pp. 273–275.

in stepping up to the plate as allies and partners in dismantling a system that we continue to benefit from.

Classism is a few decades behind the others as a very visible movement with a clear articulation of what this form of oppression means. Outside of the socialist circles in the US (which have gained some strong acceptance, approval, and even enthusiasm among the wider public in the past year; thank you, Mr. Sanders) and income sharing, egalitarian intentional communities, it seems that a lot less work has been done to articulate what classism means. As economic justice organizations, many of whom are members of the New Economy Coalition, gain more public presence, we need to get very articulate about the effects of economic insecurity and classism on all of us, as well as what solutions we can put into place to build that new world.

And we also need to develop a strong theory of what Matt Stannard of Commonomics USA calls climate egalitarianism: finding the solutions to the climate crisis that do not further endanger the poor, and do not rely simply on the goodwill of wealthy people via redistributive economic programs like welfare. Instead we need serious restructuring of the fundamentals of our economic system, developing policies and cultural practices that embody both climate responsibility and economic equality and justice.

The intentional communities movement has a role in all of this. We are offering a platform in which deep issues (like race, class, and gender) can be both dialogued about in a mature, deliberative way, and worked on through creating a new system with different power relationships between groups and individuals than our current ones.

But the movement can do that only if it takes on its own internal anti-racism and anti-classism work. Many intentional communities have simply replicated the wider culture's norms and thinking when it comes to race and class. I have some real hope, however, that it doesn't have to be that way.

Some of that hope comes from the work of communities like the Catholic Worker Houses. This network of 245 intentional communities around the world was shaped by the work of socialist and Christian, Dorothy Day. Day is best known for her activism in the 1930s around economic justice during the Great Depression. Today, the communities she inspired "remain committed to nonviolence, voluntary poverty, prayer, and hospitality for the homeless, exiled, hungry, and forsaken. Catholic Workers continue to protest injustice, war, racism, and violence of all forms."[87]

The anti-racism group I was a part of along with another dozen communitarians from northeastern Missouri worked in part from materials developed by the Catholic Workers in St. Louis, Missouri. This network continues to be at the front edge of justice work in many cities around the country and doesn't seem too inclined to rest on old work so much as engage in developing new tools for communitarians and non-communitarians alike.

---

[87] www.catholicworker.org.

Dorothy Day speaks to this urge for justice, as well as the need for communities and other radical economic structures, here quoted in *The Catholic Worker*, January, 1972:

> We will never stop having breadlines at Catholic Worker houses. ...But I repeat: Breadlines are not enough, hospices are not enough...we need communities of work, land for the landless, true farming communes, cooperatives and credit unions. There is much that is wild, prophetic, and holy about our work—it is that which attracts the young who come to help us. But the heart hungers for that new social order wherein justice dwelleth.

So yes, I have hope for the intentional communities movement playing a deeper role in racial and economic justice. I think it aligns well with the fundamental nature of community, even while it means questioning some of how our communities actually operate. We do not need to be perfect embodiments of this to contribute (that need for perfection before acting is an ego trap that lots of activists fall into) but we do need to be brave enough to recognize the importance of the work, and that it is not at all tangential to what we are doing in the movement, but rather central.

My hope stems in part from seeing the preponderance of women in leadership and visionary work within the communities movement: we have made major strides in creating a different culture around gender, and we can do the same thing in these other areas. Not that we are done with our work around gender, by any stretch of the imagination. I know of any number of communities currently grappling with deep gender dynamics, as well as ones who haven't yet reached the "grappling" stage.

As discussed earlier, income sharing groups have made especially good strides by undoing some of the economic underpinnings of sexism in our system—in other words, by valuing "domestic" labor equally with "income" labor, income sharing groups enjoy a significantly leveled playing field between men and women, and even in the least conscious of these communities, there's a palpable difference in respect and valuing of women. Still, rape culture and other dehumanizing aspects of the wider world permeate a lot of places, including our otherwise relatively safe and progressive bubbles of intentional communities.

I invite and look forward to hearing more men in the communities movement write about dismantling sexism in communities; as a middle class white woman, I am committed to doing what I can as an ally for people of color, and for working class and poor people within the communities movement, as well as within the climate justice movement.

Emotional Integration: from Paralysis to Action

In *Collapsing Consciously*, Carolyn Baker says: "we must prepare for a very uncertain future by consciously cultivating emotional resilience." I've been though my own journey around that in the past five years as climate change has slowly become more real for me. Here's one story from my own life.

It is April 2015: I'm in a B&B in Greensboro, North Carolina, on one of the rare days off during a national speaking tour. I've been talking nonstop about community and climate change for six weeks, and the emotional intensity has caught up with me. I'm a wreck, and in my isolation, I'm dealing with it with alcohol.

I've been pushing the message that one of the most critical things we need to do right now is the emotional work around planetary devastation. When we put our attention on climate change, and leave it there long enough to notice what is present for us emotionally, most of us come right up against a soul-numbing blend of anger, fear, grief, and (if we are from one of the countries that has contributed a lot to the crisis) guilt and shame.

On the tour, I've placed myself squarely on the front lines of that emotional crisis. At home, surrounded by my ecovillage friends, the emotional content is easier to handle. I have people around me who don't think I'm nuts for feeling, deeply, the grieving of the losses: the loss of the forests and oceans, the potential loss of my children's full and healthy lives, the loss of direct communion with the natural world. I have people around me who feel the anger, the fear, and the guilt, but are doing something with it other than putting their heads in the sand. I have people around me who have committed their lives to doing something about it.

At the B&B, I'm surrounded by human beauty: antiques, a lovely old farmhouse, gracious hosts. And it is illusory, the best expressions of a world built on the unreality of an economic and values system that is destroying us. I am profoundly isolated in this place, in spite of being in a city of nearly 300,000 fellow humans. I'm caught and sinking fast: deeply connected to the emotions, and alone in dealing with them.

And that is the dilemma of the American heart right now. How do we deal with profound sorrow, anger, and fear without a structure of community to hold us? How do we stay present with the emotions long enough to move through them and return to clear thinking, in time to head off the worst of the crisis, when we are still caught in it being uncool and impolite to even talk about it?

Sobonfu Somé says, "When you do not have community, you are not listened to; you do not have a place you can go and feel that you really belong."[88] I felt that lack acutely on tour. While my work during those long months was very much in service to humanity, the isolation was soul-killing. My ability to deal with my own emotions (let alone support others in dealing with theirs) eroded during that process.

---

[88] Sobonfu Somé, *The Spirit of Intimacy: Ancient African Teachings in the Ways of Relationships* (New York: Quill, 1999), p. 22.

And that's bad news, because unfortunately, we have to deal with the emotional stuff: unresolved emotions severely inhibit your ability to think clearly. In fact, it is biologically impossible to be logical and freaked out at the same time. Turning once again to the brain science experts:

> When there is any fear or anxiety the amygdala region of the brain, your emotional center, jumps to attention and takes resources away from the executive decision making of the prefrontal cortex. In a chain reaction the light goes out on the prefrontal cortex, your IQ drains like a cold beer going down on a hot afternoon and it's easier to put off the decision, make a bad decision or no decision at all.
>
> Matthew Lieberman, a neuroscientist has found an inverse relationship between the activation of amygdala and the prefrontal cortex. When the amygdala is active with blood and oxygen, there is less activation in the prefrontal cortex. …Any strong emotion, fear, stress, anxiety, anger, joy, or betrayal trips off the amygdala and impairs the prefrontal cortex's working memory. The power of emotions overwhelms rationality. That is why when we are emotionally upset or stressed we can't think straight.[89]

If you have been frustrated by our nation's inability to deal rationally with climate change, the above connects some of the dots on *why*. Without solid support for dealing with our emotional content,[90] most people literally can't be rational about it—and ironically, the more you think climate change is real and are willing to feel the inherent panic in the thought that the planet might be collapsing around us, the more irrational you might be.

Thus, most of us just don't think too hard about it. And our emotions around climate change put us into a state of amygdala overdrive that it is very hard to get past. Naomi Klein writes a long eloquent passage in *This Changes Everything* where she describes the myriad ways that we have gotten very good at avoiding the climate reality: we turn it into a joke, or "tell ourselves comforting stories about how humans are clever and will come up with a technological miracle," or declare ourselves too busy, or too small to be effective. She continues:

> Or maybe we do look—really look—but then inevitably we seem to forget. Climate change is like that; it's hard to keep it in your head for very long. We engage in this odd form of on-again-off-again ecological amnesia for perfectly rational reasons. We deny because we fear that letting in the full reality of this crisis will change everything. And we are right.[91]

---

[89] Relly Nadler Psy.D., M.C.C. "Where Did My IQ Points Go?" *Psychology Today* Apr. 29, 2011. www.psychologytoday.com/blog/leading-emotional-intelligence/201104/where-did-my-iq-points-go.

[90] I regularly ask people in my workshops how many people had a class in either cooperation or emotional intelligence in school. While Millennials occasionally put their hands up, or those who went to a Waldorf school or something similar, the vast majority have been schooled almost entirely in how to compete, rather than how to cooperate.

[91] Klein, *This Changes Everything*, pp. 3–4.

In this practice of studiously not dealing, we stay locked into half-repressed, amygdala overdrive, in a place of deep irrationality that is literally killing people and our non-human companions on this planet at an alarming rate. I have referred to this before as intergenerational genocide, and as dramatic as that sounds, I do not believe that is overstating things. As some of the biggest contributors to climate disruption, I believe we in the US have a unique obligation to get it together sooner rather than later. That means dealing with our emotions.

We have role models and teachers out there to help with this. Joanna Macy has been doing what she styles The Work that Reconnects for a long time, and Carolyn Baker, whom I quote in a number of places, is a delightfully irascible articulator of what needs to happen to pull our heads out of the sand. And the companion workbook to this book provides a number of exercises related to ending climate denial and getting the emotional support we need.

My own commitment to this work has exposed me to some sobering stories. One woman who came to one of my Encountering Climate Change workshops (designed to provide space for dealing with the emotional content around climate issues) told the group a story about hearing about ecological crisis as a child from a teacher, being terrified and going into a state of emotional overwhelm and freeze. She realized during the workshop that this incapacitation lasted for nearly four decades and caused her to be unable to live up to her own ecological ethics.

I heard echoes of her story from a number of people during the time that I was on the road talking about climate. The conclusion I came to is that we can't just throw the science and disaster predictions into people's laps without pairing that with the emotional support—it is just too crippling.

When we are able to be authentic about the emotions, and not go into hiding, some amazing activism can come of it. Bruno Seraphin again, on the Hoopsters: "The Hoopsters need to be commended for grappling emotionally with climate change—not denial, not despair either. Denial and despair are 80% of how people are responding. It's not blind hope—it fills their hearts with sorrow, grief, and rage, but they are engaging in a very active way and trying to think strategically about what this crisis can mean for the future of human beings and non-human beings."[92]

Whether the Hoopsters are an appealing model to you or not, the process that Bruno is describing here is essential: let our hearts be filled with the full experience and knowing of what we are facing, find community to support us in that, and then act strategically.

The Need for Passion

One of the other unfortunate side effects of growing up in the culture we have is a kind of deadening of our emotional bodies: it is dangerous to get

---

[92] From our interview of Nov. 16, 2016.

either too angry or too excited about anything. In *The Tao of Fully Feeling*, therapist Pete Walker provides this succinct summary:

> Unfortunately, in this culture only the "positive" polarity of any emotional experience is approved or allowed. This can cause such an avoidance of the "negative" polarity, that at least two different painful conditions result. In the first, the individual injures and exhausts himself in compulsive attempts to avoid some disavowed feeling, and actually winds up more stuck in it, like the archetypal clown whose frantic efforts to free himself from a piece of fly paper, leave him more immobilized and entangled. In the second, repression of one end of the emotional continuum often leads to a repression of the whole continuum, and the individual becomes emotionally deadened.

Passion can arise from either end of the emotional spectrum—from intense excitement and interest in something or from righteous fury at what is wrong in the world. But passion doesn't really live in the flattened center of the emotional spectrum.

The problem with this is two-fold: First, activism requires of us a clear, crisp identification of the real problems facing our world, and without access to our anger, it is hard to do that in a really authentic way. To witness injustice and live in a cultural context where it isn't OK to be with our anger is crippling.

Second, passion is a battery pack. What you are passionate about spurs you to action. If you are passionate enough and the stakes are high enough, you will risk your personal safety for it. Without that battery pack, it is hard to stay motivated to keep working for days, months, and years on making real change happen.

Passionate people are alive people—they are interesting, inspiring, and (when they have the skills to back it up) can spur others to action. Without passion, none of Joanna Macy's three-part social movement model gets very far. Without passion, we have trouble staying committed to doing our worldview-changing work, our holding actions lack oomph, and we run out of gas long before our systems have gotten changed.

Thus, one piece of our work is simply learning to be comfortable accessing the outer range of our emotional capacity. To feel deep joy, unbridled excitement, as well as deep sorrow and righteous fury is to come back alive emotionally, our batteries recharged to do our work.

Personal, Communal, and Systemic

This cultural conversation plays out in three distinct spheres: the personal, the communal, and the systemic. *Distinct*, however, should not be confused with *separate* or *unconnected*.

Personal work is part of changing the culture: the questioning of assumptions about what a good life is, what is valuable to us, how we can best interact with our fellow humans. And after the questioning starts the real work of unlearning what the mainstream culture has taught us about success and what it means to be good and a host of other things, followed by a relearning of the new paradigm. This alone is lifelong work if you take it seriously. And all of this can happen within the small sphere of our own consciousness. We carry culture in a personal way, and when we pass it on to others, it is the version we carry internally that we have to share.

Then there is the communal level of culture change work, the interpersonal sphere where we practice and learn and discover what pieces we can't look at alone because they intimately involve other people. This happens in community—some version of it or another. Culture is expressed through communication, through exchange, through education, and all of those require us to be in relationship. Some of the hardest work we will do in our culture change work arises because we hurt and betray each other, and, when those hurts and betrayals are not intentional (which I believe is most of the time) we can't know we've done so unless others speak up. Our most intimate and vulnerable culture change work happens here, at the communal level.

And then there is systems change. This is the place where the most powerful, broadly impactful structures of our culture are changed. We are caught within them, at effect of them. The law, mass communication, our economic structure, international relations, and the military—all of these are expressions of cultural values, as well as shapers of culture. They feel overwhelming to most of us, and that is because they are. It is as if we are at the center of a three-layered circle, with the personal inside, the communal surrounding that, and the broad systems we live within surrounding that.

"You can't fight the system" is wrong, but it speaks eloquently to the hopelessness we can feel in the face of forces so large. If we can change those systems, the ripple effects of those changes are tremendous. They set the stage for easier communal change and personal change, and therefore are worth the tremendous effort, the generations-in-the-making persistence to finally take a brick out of that implacable wall of oppressive culture.

If we could separate the personal and communal from that big picture, I gladly would stay in my smaller bubbles for the rest of my life. But we can't. The personal may not always be political, but the opposite isn't true: the political is always personal, and always communal. We face an uphill climb with changing the context that we form our communities within. But the regulatory environment can be changed in some places and has been changed in other places as well. The next chapter attempts to lay out the hope that it can be, the pathway we can follow, and the basic roadmap of where we are headed.

Chapter 6: Context Matters:
Legal and Economic Reform to Restore the Commons

"It's all about me, screw the Commons," is the mantra of modernity.
—Carolyn Baker, *Collapsing Consciously*

I was first introduced to the work of Brandy Gallagher at a communities conference in Seattle in 2007. The community she founded, O.U.R. Ecovillage in British Columbia, had gotten a reputation for being very savvy at working with local code enforcement officers, and the mantra that came out of that work was simple: "A 'no' is just an uneducated 'yes.'"

Brandy and her companions had ventured into the often intimidating and always time-consuming territory of the law, and had come out of it eight years later as a leader in the patient work of regulatory reform. Their local community now boasts a kind of "Ecovillage Zoning"—the first I am aware of that allows for ecovillages to do their thing as easily as it allows single-family homes occupied by nuclear families to get developed everywhere in North America. And that development designation—with the mouthful of a name, "nonprofit community services multi-stakeholder incorporated cooperative"—is regularly referred to all over Canada by both regulators and local people wanting to start communities.

Ecovillage Zoning is something the rest of the world needs, desperately. I've seen project after project burn out, essentially because our codes are based on a culture that emphasizes personal property rights to the near exclusion of cooperative endeavors, and very few intentional communities have the legal expertise and money to be able to fight their individual battles. Communities that do fight this version of the good fight are often communities that start even deeper in debt than they would otherwise simply because it can take many years and a lot of legal fees to win some of those battles. And that debt can further hinder their long-term viability. Thus, I advocate for this work to happen more at a movement level instead of each community fighting their own isolated battles.

Simply put, the context that communities operate within makes a huge difference in terms of how hard or easy it is to get the project off the ground, and can make or break a project.

I spoke in the fall of 2016 to the Boulder City Council, which was on its second pass considering an ordinance that would legalize cooperative houses within city limits. It was a high-stakes set of meetings: if it didn't pass, it would functionally render co-ops illegal in city limits, and the co-opers in town would lose their rights to their homes.

I've mentioned the Boulder scene before, back in the chapter on carbon footprints of communities. In a bigger picture, what was at stake was citizen choice to have lower carbon footprints, and thus, these small battles that happen at the municipal level, and the legal precedents they set, add up to big consequences for the planet.

I care deeply about people having the ability to choose what kind of life they want to live, including in intentional communities. This care also extends to caring about people all over the planet for whom our choices here in America (and the choice made by others in countries that have imitated us, or been pushed by the economic powers-that-be into an American-style economy and lifestyle[93]) have meant that they can no longer practice their traditional or chosen ways of life because of climate disruption.

I resist dealing with financial and legal stuff as much as the next person. And yet, if we want the options that I am talking about in this book to become widespread, I've reluctantly come to the conclusion that we need to act for extensive legal and economic reform for that to be possible. That makes Brandy Gallagher an important role model for the movement.

Brandy's Story

Brandy Gallagher grew up on a commune in the '60s and was raised by draft resisters to be socially and ecologically conscious, and not afraid to wade into controversy.[94] Talking to Brandy is a refreshing kind of real that seems to come naturally to second-generation "community kids." She is also a terrifically integrated example of leading with curiosity—that all-important skill I highlighted in the last chapter.

Brandy considers her most important lifework thus far to have been her willingness to "take on all the legal work and continuously carry that torch for our community. In some ways, I did this because no one else was willing to do it…the resistance to legal work is a subset of us that are hellbent on not doing it because we are told we are supposed to do it." Having grown up in alternative environments, she sees and understands the rebelliousness that many of us (myself included) feel when presented with a potentially long-term legal battle whose whole purpose is to allow us to simply do what we

---

[93] See Naomi Klein's *The Shock Doctrine* (Toronto: Random House of Canada, 2007) to better understand the international dynamics of neoliberal economics being forced on countries.

[94] Information in this section was gleaned from the O.U.R. Ecovillage website (ourecovillage. org), and an interview with Brandy on Nov. 21, 2016.

intuitively and factually know to be the right thing for the planet and the people we are trying to create community with.

She calls it a "red tape allergy," but is also sympathetic to the desire to avoid the legal stuff.

Harking back to the disintegration of western culture I talked about in the last chapter, she says, "We've all been enculturated into living in a fractured reality and not self-designing. We contract out our health, our food, our children's learning. We outsource our lives and get professionals to do it for us. It is almost like we've lost the theory of how to design legal systems that are based on holistic or integral systems of life, and make comprehensive plans for living." For Brandy, the legal system must be integrated just like everything else we are doing to get to a place of having truly integrated lives; leave that piece out and you are failing to embody a critical piece of the puzzle.

Not dealing with the legal frameworks around our communities means retaining some aspects of that western cultural disintegration, and remaining at effect of the values of that culture. And that just doesn't work if we really want to create a new culture. We need legal frameworks that embody our values. She likens the common avoidance to "grabbing food at McDonald's when you are a health food nut on the way to a justice meeting."

She also says that avoiding the law out of an urge for simplicity is misguided and just won't work these days. "Life is complex and rich—it isn't about going back to the land and a simple life." That's no longer timely—she says we are about 100 years too late, what with a lot of new technology, and a legal framework based more around profit motive than sustainability and care. We need to be OK with complexity. Nature is extremely complex, with interdependent systems and constant evolution. While the underlying values and principles in the legal system may be relatively simple, the processes, she says, are not. The need to engage may seem like a ginormous bummer for those of us who would just as soon not think about it, but as Brandy and I talked about her long journey as a policy reform advocate, I actually found my own interest stirring. A lot of what she said was surprising and valuable advice.

Brandy asked me a fascinating question: "Do we resist the law and think it is bad, or do we see it as a possibility that it is something that needs our help and needs healing?" Regulatory reform is an exciting challenge if we lead with curiosity about how to put the puzzle together. If we do that, at least some of us may find we suddenly have the juice to do it.

As a permaculture teacher, Brandy uses the framework of permaculture to think about designing regulatory systems. She says the goal is to take the initial "no" from regulators, and then work diligently on building long-term, authentic relationships with them that are characterized by mutual learning and problem solving. She is clear that this isn't about cozying up to officials in order to get your way, but is really about seeing them as human, and seeing regulations as serving a critical purpose: in the case of building codes, they are there to keep us safe, protect affordability and the environment, and guarantee that buildings last. Those values are all values we can get behind (and in fact are ones that natural building has a proven track record of around the world). Finding this common ground and dialoguing from that place is critical to Brandy's approach.

In fact, she emphasizes that when you go looking for examples to show regulators, there are some basic principles to follow: find multiple examples, not just one, and look worldwide; and respect their need for hard data, not just feel-good anecdotes. They have an important and hard job to do, and just as you would try to help a friend do their job well, you can help your local regulators do their job well.

One concrete example Brandy gave me was related to the number of people on a property, a common and very predictable question you will get from your land use officials when you start seeking permission to build your community. "They ask that question because of, say, transportation issues. How are people going to get in and out? A bus? They are probably going to be driving their cars, and that brings with it a whole host of issues" including street maintenance, impact on neighbors, road widths, etc. And then there are legal access issues and emergency vehicles needing to get in and out and being able to turn around properly, etc. You also need to see if it is not going to infringe on neighbors. "Those are all super valid questions," she says. "I'm grateful we were put to the test with that because we HAVE had a fire on the property."

And here's the other key: to go from "no" to a "yes" isn't good enough for a regenerative, cooperative culture. The members of Brandy's community are also looking at how to take care of not just themselves but their neighbors. For instance, in the course of the access conversations, they realized they could be of service to the whole neighborhood by offering and agreeing that they can drain the community lakes for fire suppression to help anywhere in the neighborhood. Thus, they went from a barrier to a solution to actually being a contributor to the wider community. Brandy calls this, "No to yes to yes plus."

And we very much need to be able to embody this ethic of transforming no into yes plus. "Right now, Land Use law is the biggest barrier to sustainable land development in North America, along with the very long list of other regulatory barriers." If we truly want to do the work to create the world we envision, we need US champions for regulatory reform, too, and a clear set of policy changes we are seeking.

Before I get to that policy platform, we need to look at one more piece: economics.

The Reality of Economic Insecurity

Climate disruption is, of course, not the only thing that keeps us up at night, our amygdalas over-amped and minds running in unproductive circles.

The Permaculture Principles Brandy Uses in Her Work:

Central to permaculture are the **three ethics**: care for the earth, care for people, and fair share. They form the foundation for permaculture design and are also found in most traditional societies. Here are the 12 principles of permaculture as described by David Holmgren.

1. **Observe and Interact:** "Beauty is in the mind of the beholder." By taking the time to engage with nature we can design solutions that suit our particular situation.

2. **Catch and Store Energy:** "Make hay while the sun shines." By developing systems that collect resources when they are abundant, we can use them in times of need.

3. **Obtain a Yield:** "You can't work on an empty stomach." Ensure that you are getting truly useful rewards as part of the working you are doing.

4. **Apply Self-Regulation and Accept Feedback:** "The sins of the fathers are visited on the children of the seventh generation." We need to discourage inappropriate activity to ensure that systems can continue to function well. Negative feedback is often slow to emerge.

5. **Use and Value Renewable Resources and Services:** "Let nature take its course." Make the best use of nature's abundance to reduce our consumptive behavior and dependence on non-renewable resources.

6. **Produce No Waste:** "Waste not, want not," or "A stitch in time saves nine." When we value and make use of all the resources that are available to us, nothing goes to waste.

7. **Design from Patterns to Details:** "Can't see the forest for the trees." By stepping back, we can observe patterns in nature and society. These can form the backbone of our designs, with the details filled in as we go.

8. **Integrate Rather than Segregate:** "Many hands make light work." By putting the right things in the right place, relationships develop between those things and they work together to support each other.

9. **Use Small and Slow Solutions:** "Slow and steady wins the race," or "The bigger they are, the harder they fall." Small and slow systems are easier to maintain than big ones, making better use of local resources and producing more sustainable outcomes.

10. **Use and Value Diversity:** "Don't put all your eggs in one basket." Diversity reduces vulnerability to a variety of threats and takes advantage of the unique nature of the environment in which it resides.

11. **Use Edges and Value the Marginal:** "Don't think you are on the right track just because it's a well-beaten path." The interface between things is where the most interesting events take place. These are often the most valuable, diverse, and productive elements in the system.

12. **Creatively Use and Respond to Change:** "Vision is not seeing things as they are but as they will be." We can have a positive impact on inevitable change by carefully observing and then intervening at the right time.

Economic insecurity (though it be caused by the same crazed economic system as climate disruption) is actually a much more immediate stress for many of us. Carolyn Baker paints the picture thus in *Collapsing Consciously*, pp. 25–26:

> Americans and billions of others throughout the world are…terrified about their economic future. …They are frightened about how they are going to feed their families, where they will live after losing their house to foreclosure, where they might find employment in a world where having a full-time job is becoming increasingly rare, how they will access health care without insurance or the money to pay out of pocket, and how they will make ends meet in forced or voluntary retirement. …
>
> Their immediate reality is an anomalous deprivation, a stark loss of the familiar, and the looming reality that things will not get better, but only worse. These losses are unpredictably punctuated with frightening events such as extreme weather, natural disasters, nuclear meltdowns, or the terrifying consequences of rotting infrastructure, such as pipeline explosions or collapsing bridges. These realities take their toll on the body—sleepless nights, a weakened immune system, moodiness, anger, depression, despair, and, often, suicidal thinking.

In this passage, Carolyn is simply putting a human face on the fully 55% of the American population who currently don't have enough savings to cover a $500 emergency. It helps us understand why working class white men are currently killing themselves in record numbers, and why white men, for the first time in the history of our recording such data, are starting to have shorter lifespans than their fathers.

We are a downwardly mobile society, whatever the American success myth tells us should be true. According to the University of Chicago's 40-year-long General Social Survey, only about a third of adults aged 18–35 think they are part of the US middle class and 56.5% of this age group call themselves working class—and that is a significant contraction of the middle class.

One definition of **economic security** is being able to cover your basic needs without public assistance. Only 55% of Americans meet that standard, and it is worse for people of color, women, and single people. As one example, only 18% of single mothers meet that standard. And the trend is getting worse: less than 13% of full-time jobs by 2018 will provide enough to meet it.[95]

Part of why we can't meet our needs is that lack of savings: with only 14% of the population having over $10,000 in the bank, very few people have much of a cushion, and societal safety nets seem to always be on the chopping block politically.[96]

This general downward mobility is part of the reason that making it easier to live communally, through legal reform and incentives, is so critical. The

---

[95] As reported in the *New York Times*, 2015.

[96] Stats from GOBankingRates.com.

other part is that it is hard to contemplate saving the planet when you can barely feed your kids. This is a large part of why people who work in the fossil fuel industry are fighting the reality of climate change so hard: as Naomi Klein said earlier, accepting this reality would change everything, and one needs security in order to be able to rationally contemplate change.

Somehow, we have to bring economics and ecological justice together. So far, we aren't doing very well with that.

Materializing Empathy

In 2015, Matt Stannard coined the term "climate egalitarianism" meaning:

> Solutions to the climate crisis must always account for its impact on poor and working class communities; and, conversely, programs to help those working families must always take environmental impacts into account. This commitment will require us moving beyond the redistributive policies of traditional liberal economics into policies that fundamentally restructure our economic system.[97]

This concept is essential because ecological degradation is currently coming with a disproportionate impact on the poorest among us. On top of that, many of the proposed climate "solutions" only make that problem worse. Matt believes we can do better, and so do I.

Examples of this ecological and economic mismatch abound; it is no longer just the classic owls versus logging scenario that was the go-to example in the early days of my ecological activism. From high taxes on carbon that would leave poor people without an ability to get to work because of high gas prices,[98] to geo-engineering schemes that would result in the northern (wealthier) hemisphere surviving while the southern (generally poorer) hemisphere becomes an utterly uninhabitable wasteland,[99] to the idea of powering your (expensive) electric car with your (expensive) solar panels, proposed "solutions" often treat the poor as invisible and expendable.

Matt holds a law degree from the University of Wyoming, and has been working for advocacy groups devoted to cooperative economics for several years. What he thinks we need to do instead is "materialize our empathy": create legal and material solutions that *hardwire* our deep care for one another in concrete structural ways. In this, he echoes Brandy's take on how to put together good zoning and building policies: by leading with social and environmental care and building up from there.

---

[97] Personal comunication, Jan. 2017.

[98] Fortunately, not all proposals to use an economic incentive are entirely class-clueless. The most active and notable example is the work of Citizens' Climate Lobby, who propose a carbon fee and dividend plan where we would tax carbon when it comes out of the ground, but then distribute that money directly back to the US population. This helps blunt the otherwise disastrous effects of the policy on the poor.

[99] *The Atlantic*, July/August 2009, "Re-Engineering the Earth"; Naomi Klein, *This Changes Everything*, p. 260.

Wendell Berry has said, "If we are looking for insurance against want and oppression, we will find it only in our neighbors' prosperity and goodwill and, beyond that, in the good health of our worldly places, our homelands. If we were sincerely looking for a place of safety, for real security and success, then we would begin to turn to our communities—and not the communities simply of our human neighbors but also of the water, earth, and air, the plants and animals, all the creatures with whom our local life is shared."[100]

If we are going to create the kind of commons-based, community-grounded security Berry is talking about, we need changes in our regulatory and policy environment. What would that actually look like? Matt and I have developed a public policy platform that has in mind the kinds of legal initiatives that would support citizen-led, local control of resources—of which intentional communities are one manifestation. I've expanded on that platform below, in part inspired by Bhutan (which I will talk about in Chapter 7).

Nationally, we must support efforts to:

1. *Reform our system of elections and policy-making to reduce the influence of big money in politics and expand our options.*
   - Overturn Citizens United, and make elections publicly-funded with a cap on election spending.
   - Lacking the prior two, institute a required recusal policy: if a candidate derived more than 1% of their total campaign support from any one company or industry, they may not vote on bills related to their sponsors.
   - Bring UN observers to monitor all national elections to insure fairness and reduce the likelihood of cheating.
   - Expand debate and ballot access beyond the two party system, and enact instant runoff voting.
   - Define human rights and ecological standards that all new policy proposals must meet (or at a minimum not violate) in order to be considered by legislatures, with a non-partisan evaluation board for determining what meets the criteria for consideration by the legislature. (See the Appendix on Gross National Happiness for an example of this.)

   All of these items are about power: who has it and what it is used for in our political process. Right now the bulk of the power in this country is related to money, which means it is held and wielded on behalf of those who are very good at playing the capitalism game. Capitalism is a fundamentally extractive system: it extracts wealth from the planet and labor from the people, and instead of compensating the masses for that extraction, it derives profit from it. We need to interrupt that basis for power and place it squarely in the laps of the people, whose interests

---

[100] Wendell Berry, "Racism and the Economy" in *The Art of the Commonplace: The Agrarian Essays*, edited by Norman Wirzba (Berkeley, CA: Counterpoint LLC, 2003), p. 59.

are much more diverse than simply continuing to accrue profit for a small number of people. All these electoral reforms are a variation on the theme of that interruption and re-placement of power.

2. *Enact strong federal action and international cooperation on climate change.*
   - Enact a carbon fee and dividend policy, like the one advocated for by Citizens' Climate Lobby.
   - Ban fracking.
   - End fossil fuel extraction leases on federal and state land.
   - Bring indigenous people in the US and elsewhere into the leadership of climate policymaking.
   - Replace fossil fuel subsidies with subsidies for green energy, urban and organic agriculture, carbon sequestration projects, and ecovillage development.
   - Mandate that working families who are displaced by the closure of fossil fuel production facilities be provided economic security as they transition into new lives.
   - Deepen, expand, and make permanent tax breaks for household and neighborhood scale ecological development (including solar and wind electric systems, water catchment, and green building) and ecological practices (such as public transit use, organic agriculture, working from home, and being part of a car share program).

   These suggestions are a combination of stopgap measures (redistributive economics using market forces, in the case of carbon fee and dividend, and taking care of economically displaced families), drawing healthy boundaries with the extractors, and fundamental worldview shifts (bringing indigenous wisdom into the center of policy making and supporting the building of alternative communities).

3. *Preserve and expand the Commons.*
   - End fossil fuel extraction leases on federal and state land.
   - Protect and fully fund national and state park systems.
   - Provide incentives to states, counties, cities, and community organizations that engage in land preservation and reforestation.
   - Significantly invest in less fossil fuel-intensive transportation systems, such as upgrading the US rail system and providing clean energy powered charging stations for electric cars.
   - For the public benefit, reverse the trend of privatization of services and needs; this would include (but not be limited to) ending the private prison system, unhooking health coverage for the masses from private companies, and moving all financial services from the private sector to the public in the form of public and postal banks.

   The restoration of the health and vitality of the Commons is an essential building block in the worldview and systems shifts I've been talking about in this book. Privatization is the increasing default answer to our problems, but it simply makes things worse by putting more and more of the fate of resources and people in the hands of a profit-driven system. We've significantly eroded the health of our land, air, and water, and the focus on the Commons is an effort to preserve what we still have and move toward something that is, at its core, restorative instead of extractive.

4. *Enact national economic sustainability policies.*
   - Reinstate postal banking and ban high-interest, predatory lending.
   - Shift governmental funding from fossil fuel subsidies and excessive military buildup to guaranteed basic income and the subsidies and incentives listed in this overall platform.
   - Redefine full-time employment as 30 hours per week.
   - Pass living wage laws.
   - Fully legalize and otherwise support in law local currencies and barter systems.
   - Provide support for local economy-building through things like farmers' markets, community supported agriculture, cooperative businesses, and downtown redevelopment based on local businesses.

   As our economy is becoming more automated, and there are fewer jobs to go around, we need to rethink the basic structure of how we acquire money—or more essentially, how we get our basic needs met. We should be looking at how to provide transitional support for people to be able to make the leap to getting their needs met through sharing, developing DIY skills, and stepping into barter and mutual credit networks, while insuring adequate income to get dollar-based needs met. This also marks a major shift from competitive institutions (the military and fossil fuel industry) toward cooperative ones (community and large-scale socialization) for getting our security needs met.

5. *Make it easier to get our healthcare needs met without political games involved.*
   - Establish single-payer healthcare at the federal level, and include substantial support for preventative medicine and mental health.
   - Guarantee family and sick leave for all workers.
   - Legalize marijuana.
   - Disconnect medical research from profit motive, and expand research on traditional indigenous medicines and other herbal remedies that can be grown and harvested directly by users.

   This one harks back to the section on resilience—it is hard to bounce back when the body and mind are struggling. While the exact numbers are somewhat in question,[101] it may be as high as 64% of total bankrupt-

---

[101] I'd suggest Googling this and looking for whatever Snopes' latest rundown is on those numbers. When I looked, they had concluded that the case could be made for the oft-cited 643,000 bankruptcies per year in the US. But the article itself was inconclusively fascinating.

cies in the US are caused by (or significantly contributed to by) medical debt. Lack of good healthcare is one of the most effective ways to keep a populace disempowered—we will all have an easier time building the world we want if we have a healthcare system that actually has our backs.

6. *Reform education policy.*
   - Establish and fund science-based public education on the relationship between the economy and the environment.
   - Address race, class, gender, disability, and other power differentials between people, communities, and nations as a fundamental feature of our education system.
   - Bring back fundamental skills building (such as carpentry, gardening, cooking, and first aid), provide deeper arts funding, and introduce emotional intelligence and cooperation teachings for all students.
   - End property tax-based school funding differentials and establish a constitutional right to adequately funded education.
   - Make public universities free.

   There are three pieces to this: having good enough basic education so that we can raise the bar on public discourse (the current state of which is horrendous), recognizing the tie between education and economic empowerment at its most fundamental level (and in this I am using the word "economic" in the way I want it used: to be able to get our needs met), and recognizing the lack of education around oppression dynamics in our culture, which very much must be rectified for us to make collective progress on all of these fronts.

7. *Encode socioeconomic rights, and reform the legal system.*
   - Create and expand legally actionable rights to food, water, healthcare, housing, and a healthy environment.
   - Expand human rights and environmental law training in all law schools.
   - Provide Restorative Justice training to lawyers, judges, advocates, and police forces, and make it broadly known that victims and perpetrators alike can invoke this approach for their cases. (See also #9, below, and the Black Lives Matter platform in Appendix III.)

   The legal system is where a lot gets decided in our culture, and without the recognition of fundamental human rights, we are limited in what rights are protected. Restorative Justice is very much like a legal arm of cooperative culture. Our system is currently based on punitive thinking, not looking at the context for crime, or the relational aspects of the effects of crime. Reorienting how we think of justice in a legal sense is one of the many intersected pieces that we need to pay attention to to build a sustainable world.

8. *Make international policy based on fair trade and sustainability.*
   - Enact strong international fair trade and ecological standards across all borders (as well as for domestic trade).
   - Repeal laws that ban favoring local businesses.

   Naomi Klein's *Shock Doctrine* is an excellent full text exploring this area, and I highly recommend it. One of the more telling revelations in the book for me was that many international trade treaties will not allow local municipalities or businesses to favor localization, which means that it is incredibly difficult to build a local economy in any significant way. The movement for fair trade has been gaining momentum for a couple decades, but can only get so far before it bumps into international disincentives and barriers.

9. *Make serious, material efforts to restore right relationship between racial and cultural groups in the US.*
   - Provide reparations to Native American and African American people, in the form of housing and business subsidies, and other means as recommended by members of both groups.
   - Recognize the sovereignty of indigenous tribes, and treat them as international partners in all negotiations that affect their land, livelihood, and way of life.
   - Adopt the Black Lives Matter platform in full (see Appendix III for the full platform; it is summarized here, minus things that are covered elsewhere in this platform).

   This one is simple: if the world doesn't materially work for everyone, then it is failing. American capitalism has relied for its survival on extracting wealth from native lands and black bodies (among other oppressed populations) for far too long. It isn't enough to change systemic oppression (though that is absolutely needed): we need to pair reform with making a good-faith effort to restore deeply damaged relationships based on centuries of that oppression.

At the local and state level, we see the need to:

1. Broaden services designed and defined as public utilities.
   - Establish state and municipal public banks, with profits reinvested in locally, democratically determined priorities.
   - Create a public utility model for legal services.

   Many cities provide services such as water, and recycling and trash pick-up. It's great to have some of these ecological-dimension services covered by a public entity. This part of the platform advocates expanding those services to meet economic- and social-dimension needs via publicly-run utilities as well. Public banks are a particularly potent example of that. Our current banking system sends a huge amount of locally generated capital to Wall Street in the form of interest and other financing payments. If even a small percentage of Wall Street's annual profits were to stay with local communities, under local democratic control, it would be a remarkable game-changer for localization efforts all over the US.

2. Support local economic autonomy.
   - Deregulate and promote local and alternative currencies, barter networks, cooperative economic initiatives, and local food production.
   - Promote and financially incentivize worker-owned, cooperative enterprises.

   In addition to the public banking strategy (above) there are many ways we can build a local economy from the ground up, one grassroots project at a time. However, the regulatory environment right now favors more traditional business models, and makes it very difficult for cooperative localization efforts to succeed.

3. Enable cooperative and sustainable community living.
   - Reform local and state codes (including banking practices and occupancy limits) to be more favorable toward cooperative living and resource sharing projects of all kinds.
   - Create state-level ecovillage development subsidies. (In the next section, I'll flesh out more fully what this means.)

   As Brandy Gallagher pointed out, the biggest barrier to community formation in many places (especially urban and suburban areas) is the law. Simply removing those barriers would be huge. However, just as we've been protecting personal property rights and the profit-making rights of individual ownership for generations, we could be using the law to plug into more cooperative and collective frameworks, protecting those rights as well (or instead).

All of Us

Returning for a moment to my five-part economic needs model (Chapter 3): this policy platform is designed in part to make it possible for everyone to fully partake in that model. It offers economic incentives for reducing our dependency on money, and radically changes the fifth part of that model—our relationship to the US dollar, when monetary exchange is the only way to meet a need. By bringing more integrity to that system, and providing for baseline income for all people, the achievement of this policy platform would allow us to get our needs met in far more ecologically and socially responsible ways.

If and when we need money, these policies would have it come from universal basic income, and living wages earned in a more humane amount of time, while decoupling things like health coverage from our jobs. Having our money handled through a combination of local currencies, and public and postal banks, eliminates a lot of problematic aspects of how money is moved and managed.

The above articulates a policy and structural framework for building the world I believe would be economically and ecologically just. Obviously no single organization is going to get this done: I recognize and celebrate the solidarity across movements and organizations that would be needed to achieve this. And just as clearly, lacking one of these pieces diminishes the potency and potential of multiple other pieces of the puzzle. Thus, even in our political action, community is a very necessary thing: just as no one person within a community will have all the skills and insights that community needs in order to do everything themselves, no one group is going to be able to handle all of this, and we really do need all the pieces to this puzzle if we are going to get the world we want.

My main focus is likely to continue to be working directly on the cultural and policy frameworks to make cooperative living possible. To that end, I've thought a lot about what state and municipal governments could do to help foster this way of life. The Boulder City Council in January 2017 passed a solidly supportive (though not quite ideal) ordinance that legalized and supported cooperatives. That's a good example of a starting place.

Going beyond simple legalization and defining, though, there could be much greater material support for this kind of living. I envision ecovillage subsidies to be an excellent way to do this. And here are the basic parameters I would use.

Require at least these three things:

1. Land held in a Land Trust, or other form of collective ownership of the land and major infrastructure.

2. Democratically control by the residents of the community.

3. Concrete targets and timelines for carbon reduction compared to the local average (or state average if local statistics are not available).

If these requirements are met, the government entity would provide financial support for:

1. Land purchases.

2. Collective infrastructure development, including both common spaces and community-owned housing, with an emphasis on ecologically responsible technologies.

3. Organic agricultural establishment.

4. Training in cooperative living and core homesteading skills.

5. Living-wage salary for a coordinator whose job would include tracking progress on carbon reduction goals and reporting those gains to the governmental agency providing the funding.

Why is this important? The communities movement is currently a largely white and middle class phenomenon, although exceptions to this are becoming both more prevalent and more widely known. One of the reasons this appears to be true is that you need a certain level of financial privilege in order to be able to be part of starting a community. Once a group is established without much racial and ethnic diversity, it becomes very difficult to get out of that box.

Most groups struggle financially and therefore have a hard time being truly financially accessible. It's hard enough, the story goes, just to get any intentional community off the ground without also trying to deal with what seem to many to be tangential issues. They are *not* tangential, and yet there is a nugget of truth in that story—intentional communities simply aren't exempt from the struggles facing the wider culture, and we can't wave a magic wand and suddenly change them. We *can* make some progress for sure within our individual communities, and absolutely should be doing so. However, the problems *are* bigger than any one group—they are society-wide and built right into the economic and regulatory framework we find ourselves in.

Thus, while middle class Americans have had much more access to the intentional community model, and have reaped more of the benefits of collective economics and social connection that community can provide. Cooperative living remains a limited tool for people dealing with economic insecurity—ironically the group who may well benefit the most from it. As an effective tool for addressing climate change and the social isolation that comes from a strongly materialistic culture, intentional communities should be part of an overall platform for addressing the intersection of economic and ecological justice.

In short, poor people should also have access to the choice to live in community.

I also see a shift in governmental support as one aspect of the cooperative culture transition I talked about in the last chapter: shifting from supporting ecologically devastating, competitive entities toward ecologically nurturing, cooperative ones would be an appropriate role for responsible government.

Policy and the Personal

> We have to abandon the conceit that isolated personal actions are going to solve this crisis. Our policies have to shift.
> — Al Gore

I've come to significantly agree with Al Gore on this. Thus the policy reform recommendations.

Part of my agreement relates to just how uphill those personal changes can be in our current cultural and regulatory environment. The truth is, a massive rebellion against hyper-consumerism would be an effective tool to shift the economic pressures that keep us locked in—but it would have to be massive. It is slowly building, but probably not fast enough. I'm arguing for a combination of changing the context for our actions, and also making the personal *communal* instead of isolated. Both of these are very much needed.

There are other reasons, though, to continue your personal actions. Chief among them is the state of your own integrity. Walking around in a constant, low-level state of feeling yourself violating your own values is stressful. With a little bit of diligence, you can make some different decisions and feel a lot more grounded. These decisions can be large (what job you have and whether it allows you to be significantly car-free or ties you to a significant daily commute) or small (the choice to buy organic when you have the money to do it), but we probably have a few hundred opportunities to make choices that relate to our carbon footprints every year. That's a lot of either guilt opportunity or ethical coherence opportunity, and at some point, how you feel about your daily choices will affect your mental health, for good or ill.

The other reason is practice, and there are two parts to this. First, we will find our choices narrowed by climate change, and being able to more gradually acclimate to them is just kinder to yourself. Second, cooperative skills take some serious time to develop, and the sooner we all get started, the better off we all will be.

So yes: policy and economics are the big-picture leverage points we need to see shifted, and I strongly encourage everyone who cares about the planet and people around you to wade into pushing for those changes. But I have little hope that the federal government is going to act quickly on these things, and waiting (whether that is passively or actively) isn't wise. We can do a lot now, both personally and collectively, to develop those systems that will replace the old paradigm, and to make viable, visible examples of ourselves for what a minimal- or post-carbon world will actually look like. We can also focus on local politics, where I think a tremendous amount can be done (witness Brandy Gallagher's experience and the recent wins in Boulder).

I'm not predicting a certain timeline here, but we could think of this as being a 10- to 20-year game we are engaged in: we have that much time to develop alternatives, make them visible, and change the regulatory framework. There's a lot of work necessary in a short period of time, on all three fronts Joanna Macy speaks of: worldview change, holding actions, and systems change.

A line from one of my favorite musicians, the fiery, smart, savvy Nahko Bear, comes to mind: "Find your Medicine, and use it." I know many of you already know what your gift is, and many are already very active. If you are, thank you. And if not, it is time to pursue that in earnest.

Chapter 7: Together Resilient

Many persons have a wrong idea about what constitutes true happiness.
It is not attained through self-gratification but through
fidelity to a worthy purpose.
—Helen Keller

Prius or Punt?

I want to bring in one more worldview piece to the worldview puzzle. It relates all the way back to one of my first footnotes in this book: does "sustainable" mean to sustain our current lifestyles, or does it mean living in a way the planet can sustain? I think it has to mean living within the planet's capacity.

And that means that we have some deep questions to ask right now about how we are living. Do we buy a more efficient car and light bulbs, and put solar panels up on our homes in order to sustain the lifestyle to which we have become accustomed? Or do we radically change the set-up of our lives so that we drive rarely and use far less electricity? That's the difference between faux sustainability and real sustainability.

It isn't that buying a hybrid is bad or that solar panels are bad. These are good technological innovations, and used within an overall system, they can be components of a solution. But they are not the solution—they are useful tools. Many of us are waiting for technology to save us from ourselves. We picture releasing mass amounts of sulfur into the air to block the fiercest of the sun's rays, or expect someone to invent a ginormous vacuum cleaner that will magically remove carbon from the air.

We hold out these hopes—this magical thinking, really—because it is easier to daydream about someone else saving the day than it is to actually look at what our lifestyles have done to the planet and consider that we might have to seriously change our ways, might have to give up some measure of our comfort and ease. Less selfishly, we feel terrible about the possibility that our children will not enjoy the kind of ease we have enjoyed, and it breaks our hearts to consider that possibility.

The prime directive of parenting for decades in the US has been: give your kids a "better" life, with "better" being defined as more materially wealthy and easeful. This drives a lot of our not thinking about climate change. Every parent I know who is taking climate change seriously, myself included, is silently praying that our kids just get a good childhood, a good life, before it all falls apart.

However, this generates a set of "solutions" that are more like pain medication than cure—more band-aid than healing. It is a combination of a consumeristic worldview and extractive economics that has gotten us here, and whatever technological fixes or other approaches we make that paper over those things will not really change what needs to be changed. Relying on technology is a lot like the redistributive economic model I talked about in the last chapter—it may shuffle things around a bit and provide some relief, but it doesn't actually solve the core problems in front of us. Just like our economic system, our ecological systems need a deeper reboot.

Here are a few thought-provoking and sobering realities from one of the more positively disturbing books that have been handed to me in recent years, *The Conundrum: How Scientific Innovation, Increased Efficiency, and Good Intentions Can Make Our Energy and Climate Problems Worse*, by David Owen. His basic premise is that increasing the efficiency of a technology can lead to the thing being used more, and actually contributes, more often than not, to increased consumption and pollution. If that Prius makes you feel righteous about driving, you might do it more. If carpool lanes and more people taking buses make commuting a more pleasant experience and easier to stomach, people commute more. This is how good technologies and innovations often result in the opposite of their intention.[102]

Owen recommends three basic guidelines for improving our ecological footprints: live smaller, live closer, and drive less. There are two places where this is easy: cities with excellent public transit and fully featured, walkable neighborhoods, and intentional communities that are similarly fully featured and encourage small living spaces by having common facilities. In other words, our sustainable future looks like either Manhattan or Twin Oaks. And if you take a page from Jifunza Carter-Wright's book, it might actually look like urban/rural partnerships between these two basic patterns. I'm advocating a cultural punt. In football, you have four chances (called downs for those who aren't familiar with American football) to move the ball at least 10 yards down the field before your chances reset. Thus, if you've tried three times, you are faced with a choice on fourth down: do you try again, or punt? Punt turns the ball over to the other team (but usually further from their end zone than if you try and fail to make a first down), and you go from playing offense to playing defense.

Anyone who follows football knows that, unless you are very, very close to meeting your goal, the safer (and more common) choice is punting rather

---

[102] This is called the Jevons paradox, and I was introduced to it in *The Conundrum* in 2012. This disturbingly smart book was handed to me by Toby Champion. Thanks. I think.

than trying one more time. So that's where we are—we've been playing offense, trying to win, trying to score for a good long while. And we find ourselves right now at a long-shot fourth down: can we make it? Or is it time to change the game and work on defending what we have instead of trying to get ahead more?

My advice: punt. Get some different players on the field and consolidate. In this case, that doesn't mean giving up, it means changing our mindset to one that is actually appropriate for where we are, and engaging new leaders, giving some new players a chance to do their part.

One more somewhat deflating fact from Owen: in America today, nearly all of us who aren't actually homeless live far better than the royalty of olden days. If you have a flush toilet, a hot shower, access to a conveyance that is temperature controlled, and food that can get to your table more cheaply than supporting a full staff to fell trees, chop wood, and light fires, you have luxury unknown to monarchs a few hundred years ago. That's not said to shame anyone about what you want, but rather to convey that what we consider baseline (let alone the luxuries we work so hard for) is far beyond what was normal a couple centuries back.

Pair that though with this interesting nugget:[103] One gallon of gas contains the equivalent energy of 500 hours (that's 62.5 eight-hour days) of human labor. That seems crazy, right? I think about this sometimes while driving and it doesn't seem possible that it would take 62.5 long days of walking to go as far in my car as a gallon will take me…but then I'm also moving the weight of the car itself. I can certainly see how it could take a half dozen people 10 days to PUSH my car (plus my butt, sitting in it) 35 to 50 miles!

So fossil fuels are an incredibly powerful thing. That eight-block walk to the store that you choose to drive instead actually takes a huge amount of energy, and we do it remarkably casually.

Part of what I want to interrupt by sharing these perspectives is that casualness. Certain things are human rights: access to clean water and air, for instance. Most of what we have these days in the US, though, we literally could live without and might just possibly be happier if we did. One of my main theses in my teaching and public speaking work is that living a sustainable life doesn't suck, and can in fact be a pretty fabulous life.

So let's talk, as our closing thoughts, about happiness.

Scaling Up…Way Up

Is it possible to scale up what is happening in the intentional communities movement? Could a whole country be intentional enough to embody a carbon-free future? Tiny Bhutan, with a population of just 784,000 people, might well be an answer to that.

---

[103] David Pimentel published this calculation on the vhemt.org website, drawing on data from Louisiana Oil and Gas Association and the US Department of Energy.

Case Study Three: Bhutan[104]

A group of researchers studying variations in per capita carbon emissions notes that "Much of the U.S. resistance to ambitious global efforts to reduce carbon dioxide emissions reflects a fear common amongst Americans that high emissions are necessary to maintain high standards of living."[105]

It's worth questioning that assumption, and asking an even deeper question about how we define quality of life or a high standard of living, and to do so I'm going to invite you to take a look at this tiny Buddhist country squeezed between China, India, and Bangladesh. Bhutan is the only nation in the world that has a negative carbon footprint. They also are the nation that pioneered the concept of measuring Gross National Happiness instead of Gross National Product as their primary measure of cultural health. But they aren't measuring the "think positive thoughts" version of happiness that many Americans have become obsessed with, nor do they conflate shopping therapy with real personal growth.

They are measuring well-being, along the lines of Helen Keller's take on happiness, and have "a commitment to building an economy that would serve Bhutan's culture based on Buddhist spiritual values, instead of western material development gauged by gross domestic product."[106] Bhutan is, in fact, a Buddhist country officially (though the constitution protects the right to freedom of religion).

I don't think the constitutionally mandated attention on a non-material marker of well-being and the fact that Bhutan has the only negative carbon footprint in the world are coincidental, and neither does Pascale Aline Bertoli, a Ph.D. candidate in psychology and practicing Buddhist who has made four trips to Bhutan in the past 14 years and who spoke to me about her impressions of the country.

What struck me most strongly during our conversation was how many times I found myself thinking, "Wow…that's really similar to how intentional communities do that." Sufficiently intrigued, I found that Bhutan organically emerged as the third "case study" for this book.

The Bhutanese constitution also mandates certain ecological values, and in fact states explicitly that 60% of the country (at a minimum) shall remain in forest cover in perpetuity. Both of these things represent a country with a worldview that is explicitly anti-material, with both the ecological and well-being commitments arising from a strong spiritual basis.

In many ways, Bhutan is the large-scale answer to that question I pose to

---

[104] Please note: unlike the other two communities I've used for case studies in this book, I've never been to Bhutan personally. I expect I'm making some mistakes here, and apologize if that is the case.

[105] Elizabeth A. Stanton, Frank Ackerman, and Kristen A. Sheeran, "Why Do State Emissions Differ so Widely?" *Economics for Equity and the Environment Network*, www.e3network.org. December 2010.

[106] From Wikipedia entry on Gross National Happiness.

my students in my workshops: if you started with a more caring worldview, what social, economic, and ecological systems would arise from that worldview? In fact, GNH has four explicit pillars,[107] and in them, you can hear the integration of the four dimensions of sustainability, just as we could in the Bay Buck reasons to join:
Sustainable development.

- Preservation and promotion of cultural values.
- Conservation of the natural environment.
- Establishment of good governance.

Sustainable development is the bringing together of ecological and economic values; preservation of cultural values is where worldview meets social; conservation of the natural environment brings together worldview (conservation being a philosophy of management) and ecological; and good governance is social again. This echoes, remarkably well, the intersectionality of the four dimensions that inspired the Global Ecovillage Network to create the Gaia Education curriculum in the first place. And like ecovillages who do a good job of bringing all four dimensions together, Bhutan displays remarkable ecological numbers.

They've also done well by some of the most common standards of quality of life. According to the United Nations, they've seen a steady rise in both life expectancy and a formula called the Human Development Index since 1990.

By my reading, Bhutan is essentially one ginormous ecovillage, and a successful one at that. It embodies the kinds of policies I am talking about in my policy reform platform, and is therefore worth studying in and of itself. And because of that, it is also an answer to whether it is possible to scale up sustainability from the 50–100 adult scale that Dancing Rabbit and Twin Oaks are currently embodying.

An Intentional Community Analysis of Bhutan

Is it possible for a whole country to functionally be an intentional community? As someone deeply involved with the US intentional communities movement for over two decades, I can say that there are ways that Bhutan fits the mold as well as any officially designated intentional communities. The reason for me to consider it this way is that it helps us to see what is possible through a framework of deliberate, empowered action, and I think that's worth spending a bit of ink on.

The Fellowship for Intentional Community says this about communities it represents in the Communities Directory and *Communities* magazine:

> The FIC defines an intentional community as a group of people who live together or share common facilities, and who regularly associate with

---

[107] See Appendix III for a more thorough discussion of GNH. What is written above is very much a high level summary.

each other on the basis of explicit common values. In other words, it's a group of people who share things because they want to live a similar lifestyle and pursue a common ideal or vision. Conjure up your image of a traditional village and you'll have an idea of what a lot of people are going for. Obviously, in our modern world, it's a lot more complicated than traditional village life, but the aim is to have an integrated, interconnected, interdependent life with others that provides social and economic benefit as well as a place to live out other values, such as sustainability, social justice, and/or spiritual/religious tenets.

And here is one of the more popular and used definitions of an ecovillage, originally articulated by Robert Gilman:

An ecovillage is a human-scale, full-featured settlement, with multiple centers of initiative, in which human activities are harmlessly integrated into the natural world in a way that is supportive of healthy human development, and can be successfully continued into the indefinite future.

Other traditional villages have been deliberately restyled as ecovillages in recent years. The best known and largest of these is a series of about 10,000 interconnected villages in Sri Lanka that decided to embrace the ecovillage model as a way to preserve their traditional way of life and bring dignity back to villages that were starting to see major migration of young people to urban environments. So blurring the lines between still extant sustainable ways of living and "modern" ecovillages is nothing new.

Looking at the main components of both the FIC's statement on communities and the ecovillage definition, here's how I see Bhutan fitting.

Shared values that guide the community's decisions and create a unique culture. Bhutan is clearly a Buddhist country, and the precepts of Buddhism were used to develop the country's constitution, to inform the Gross National Happiness measurements, and to create their policy development criteria. Bhutan may well be one of the most thorough examples of *deliberately* using a shared worldview to permeate every aspect of life. In this way, I'd characterize Bhutan as a large-scale, very well-integrated spiritual community.

A sense of choice in participation. This one is tricky, because Bhutan is almost completely populated by people of Bhutanese descent. How much choice could there be? But there is: some people have left because they can't fit themselves into the culture easily (Pascale cited a marginalized gay friend when I asked her what the shadow is in Bhutan), and those who remain "fiercely value" the culture. Most years, Bhutan has a positive immigration rate, meaning that more people move to Bhutan than leave. There is also strong internet connectivity: this isn't a case where people have no idea that they have options.

All of that said, it is true in Bhutan, like everywhere else, that people with more money have more choices about where they live and more chances to opt out of the situation they've been born into. And even though Bhutan has a pretty narrow range of wealth compared to most places, a gap still exists. Thus, my take on this is that for this criteria, the fit isn't perfect.

Deriving benefit from and directly caring for the commons. When I asked Pascale how she would categorize decision-making and economics in Bhutan, she laughed and said it is a multi-part hybrid of multiple systems: a little capitalism, a little more socialism, mainly representative democracy, but a little top-down oligarchy still lingering from the pre-transition days. What was quite clear, though, is that there's a lot of collective management of resources and shared facilities. The monasteries play a huge role in village life, and serve as collective gathering places. There are also widespread forestry projects, many of which are strongly managed by local communities for the benefit of those communities. (There are also country-wide tree planting events, including the one many people heard about on social media in 2016 where the country planted 109,000 trees in honor of the king's son being born.) Programs managing water resources have shifted in recent years to be more based on intervillage cooperation rather than villages focusing on just taking care of their own. My assessment is that the participation in and care of the commons is very strong in Bhutan (and in fact seems to be a major factor in the country's negative carbon footprint—all those trees are a terrific carbon sequestration strategy).

Human activity harmlessly integrated into the natural world in a way that can be successfully continued into the indefinite future. Bhutan's negative carbon footprint offers good evidence that they are doing well with this. There are also other aspects to that. Pascale told me that some of the wealthiest people in the country are actually traditional nomads who work directly with the forest ecology to cultivate Cordeceps, a medicinal mushroom much prized in China. The nomads are left alone by the government, and allowed to cross into various groups' territories. (This is a bit reminiscent of the Hoopsters, except with widespread social and government acceptance.) Finally, Pascale says the culture as a whole is decidedly non-material, a "way of life completely upside down from the west." It seems to me to be very like an ecovillage at its best in terms of working with the natural world and its inherent limits, instead of trying to get around them.

A way of life supportive of healthy human development. Pascale (who, remember, is in the mental health field) tells me that one of the things that keeps drawing her back is that she sees no evidence of mental illness in the population as a whole, beyond senility associated with aging. She said that she is seeing addiction issues starting to show up in the younger people who have left the country, spent time in western cultures, and come back, but not in people who are more firmly and contentedly rooted in Bhutanese culture. The statistics on well-being and happiness also back up her observations, and I'll lay those out in the next section. Again, this seems to fit well with the definition of an ecovillage.

One last criteria I want to add, and this one comes from Elinor Ostrom's Nobel prize-winning work on functional collective resource management systems (of which I consider intentional communities to be a subset): **clear boundaries in both geography and membership.** Just as intentional communities sometimes find themselves dealing with membership expulsions, Bhutan does the same. And this dimension came up when I asked Pascale about what the "shadow" is in Bhutanese society (because frankly it sounds a little too good to be true when you read about it and hear it described by someone who loves the place).

In addition to some people (like Pascale's gay friend) voluntarily opting out of Bhutanese "membership," the Bhutanese government has gone to some fairly extreme lengths to protect the integrity of their philosophical and physical borders. In 1995, Bhutan deported a large number of people of Nepalese descent because they had been developing military bases within Bhutan to help overthrow the Nepalese government. Wanting no part of a violent overthrow of a neighboring government, the Bhutanese government threw them all out.

There are also less extreme versions of protecting the group boundaries: Bhutan strictly enforces limits on tourist traffic into the country, and then takes pains to track closely what people are doing. Again, some communities have similar practices—having a limited number of visitor slots each year, and restricting where visitors go and what they participate in. What feels reasonable as a way of protecting the home-space of the community for members looks downright oppressive when done on a country scale. And yet Ostrom says you've got to do it (or at least some version of it) if you want your members or citizens to retain good management of the commons—and, I would add, a coherent culture. Thus, I see Bhutan functioning similarly to an intentional community, albeit in one of the most difficult realms communities find themselves needing to navigate.

Overall, Bhutan appears to be a very solid match with my understanding of what it means to be an intentional community, and is a solid rebuttal to people who say that what we are doing in the movement will only ever be a fringe phenomenon with low participation numbers. Just as Dancing Rabbit and Twin Oaks provide hope that it is possible on a small scale, Bhutan is an excellent example of what is possible on a much larger scale, If nearly three quarters of a million people are successfully using these principles, there is no real reason to claim that such community isn't scalable. And of course, none of these communities are perfect: they all have shadows they are still working out, and none of them are a good fit for everyone.

But together, our three case studies describe variations on the theme: spiritual and secular; income sharing and independent; consensus, elected councils, and parliamentary democracy; Americans and Bhutanese; experimental and deeply traditional cultures. There are a lot of different ways to structure our sustainable lives. What they all have in common is a sense of being in it together, and a deep care for both people and planet.

Follow the Bliss?

It turns out that living in community is not only good for the planet, it is also good for you.

Looking back for a moment at Bhutan, the Gross National Happiness index provides a sense of what is possible at a large scale. The 2015 GNH Index survey did extensive evaluations of 7153 Bhutanese (that's about 1% of the total population of the country, and they made sure to include people from every region). From that, analysts created a GNH profile for each person, showing their well-being across all of the areas included in GNH, then used the compilation of these profiles to determine the overall GNH of the country.

The result was that 91.2% of Bhutanese are "narrowly, extensively, or deeply" happy,[108] and 43.4% of Bhutanese are "extensively or deeply" happy, which is up from 40.9% in 2010. These numbers are pretty darn good, and yet Bhutan is not content: they want everyone in the country to be at least "extensively" happy, and that is the aim of many of their policies and governmental initiatives.

Ok, so sure, happy Buddhists are common in a country that really cares about its people. For many of us, that seems like a pretty distant reality, though. How about something closer to a scale we can envision creating for ourselves?

Returning for a moment to our first case study community, Dancing Rabbit Ecovillage, anthropologist Dr. Joshua Lockyer has spent nearly a decade interacting with and studying this community. He and Brooke Jones (whose data we looked at in Chapter 2) have also done some quality-of-life evaluations of the community. Josh says this in an article in *The Journal of Political Ecology*:

> In order to assess quality of life we did a series of in person interviews with community members in which we asked questions regarding their happiness and well-being. Two quantitative, Likert scaled questions are included in the interview protocols. When asked, "How happy are you with life at Dancing Rabbit right now?" 81% of participants reported a level of 7 or above, on a scale from 1 to 10 with 1 being least happy and 10 being most happy. When asked, "Do you think Dancing Rabbit is a good place to live?" 88% of participants responded with a 4 or 5 on the following scale: 1 = not at all a good place to live, 2 = a somewhat good place to live, 3 = neutral, 4 = good, and 5 = extremely good. These results are especially interesting given the interviews were completed during a time of exceptionally high tensions within the community surrounding a

---

[108] Data from the Centre for Bhutan Studies and GNH Research, November 2015 summary of survey findings.

contentious process of reordering the community's capital expenditure budgets.

He further notes that these results are similar to what people living in Seattle—generally rumored to be a good place to live—say about their lives.

And it isn't just Dancing Rabbit. A major international study[109] recently found that life in intentional communities is generally experienced as positive. One of the more interesting tidbits was that, on a survey that included 20 distinct groups, the only people with a higher level of life satisfaction than women living in intentional communities were Norwegian women who were either pregnant or had recently given birth. Men in community also fared well, being the seventh most satisfied group, beating out college students in four countries, Australian adults and the Amish, among others.

Of the subgroups of Americans surveyed, people living in community also reported the highest degree of meaning in life:[110]

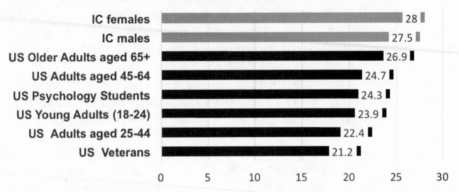

A comparison of "Presence of Meaning in Life" scores from a range of previously studied populations (Steger et al., 2006). Residents of ICs report relatively higher levels of meaning in their lives compared to the US mainstream.

Lest you think only happy people join community in the first place, a third data set from this same study provides a before and after comparison for people currently living in community. They asked if life was better or worse for the respondent since joining a community. Of the 943 people who responded to the question, 80% said that life was better or much better, with "much better" being the most common response of the seven choices. Only 1% of respondents said their lives were worse or much worse since joining a community.

In other words, if life in intentional communities was a "product" it would be getting rave reviews from "buyers."

---

[109] Data from researchers Dr. David Sloan-Wilson and Ian McDonald of Binghamton University in New York and Ragnhild Bang Nes of the Norwegian Institute of Public Health, 2015. Personal communication.

[110] Bjørn Grinde, Ragnhild B. Nes, Ian F. MacDonald, and David Sloan Wilson. In Press. "Quality of Life in Intentional Communities," *Social Indicators Research*.

This study has provided significant data to confirm what a lot of people who live in community have felt intuitively for a long time: that living with others is simply better than living alone for most of us. I'll readily admit that it is scary and weird to contemplate making this leap for most people—I've talked to too many people sitting, tortured, on the fence about it—but those who take the leap seem to be overwhelmingly happy about that choice.

What's Not to Love?

I'm not going to tell you that living in community is utopia, or simple, or easy. In fact, a cohousing friend of mine, Zev Paiss, is fond of saying that when he moved to community, his life didn't get simpler, but it did get more rich, and I think Zev probably speaks for a lot of us in this movement. I know people who never owned a weekly planner until they moved to Dancing Rabbit: it isn't about some idyllic, unscheduled pastoral scene that you suddenly find yourself painted into. You may get more support in community for your life challenges, and more skilled people around you to help you sort things out, but the old adage, "wherever you go, there you are" holds true in community just as much as out of it.

Community is not a magic wand.

What it is, instead, is a powerful tool. In the age of climate disruption, it is a tool that has the potential to save a lot of lives and preserve a lot of goodness in the world, if it is wielded skillfully.

I've tried to make the case in this book, in fact, that community can offer four incredibly timely and valuable things to people who take the plunge into communities that are well-designed:

1. Social support and an end to isolation.

2. Increased economic security, and a deepening of what security means.

3. A higher degree of life satisfaction, and congruence of values with lifestyle.

4. More easeful reduction of your carbon and ecological footprints.

Any one of these four would be a fine motivation for many people to seriously consider living more cooperatively. As we enter in earnest the age of climate disruption, all four of these seem to me to be becoming more elusive if we try to do life on our own. I believe we are entering the age where community isn't just a nice idea, or something for a privileged few, or even a choice. More and more, well-conceived, intentional, sustainability-oriented communities are an actual necessity for us to survive and possibly even thrive.

Afterword:
The Future of the Intentional Communities Movement

People glorify all sorts of bravery except the bravery they might show on
behalf of their nearest neighbors.
— George Eliot, *Middlemarch*

I said way back in the introduction that the intentional communities
movement needs to move beyond being a network of projects scattered all
over the world, and into leading some aspects of greater social change. I offer
here my challenge to my fellow communities movement activists.

We often doubt our relevance. I'm asking us to stop doing so. The world
needs us to show up: teach, lead, shape the culture. I'm constantly surprised
by how many people living in really remarkable communities go into conversations with people in the wider culture with an air of reticence and almost
shame at speaking about where they live: we've taken in too much the "flaky
hippie" talk, the "dropping out of society" talk, the "but what about the real
world" talk.

Friends, our world is in so many ways far more real than the one rep-
resented by the consumerist lifestyle. Far from being flakes, the vast majority of us are hard-working, deeply grounded, and incredibly caring people
who have figured out some really important things about how to live, how
to prosper on less, how to be more conscious and responsible humans. The
real miracle I see in the movement is how many of us have done these things
with far greater loyalty to practicality than dogma. You haven't dropped
out—you've dropped in to something incredibly powerful, and in many ways
more in touch with what is actually happening in the world than our more
mainstream companions. You've taken seriously enough the economic and
ecological challenges that are trashing the world that you've made your life
into a vessel for real change.

So—don't buy the hype about us. Claim what you know and model the
deep humility so many of you are capable of when you don't know something
and are eager to learn from other movements. But please—see yourselves as
relevant and organize as if our lives depend on it.

I'm very much afraid they do.

Appendix I: More on the Hofstede Indices

Here are the more complete descriptions of each of the Hofstede Indices I discussed in Chapter 5.[111]

Here again is the graph:

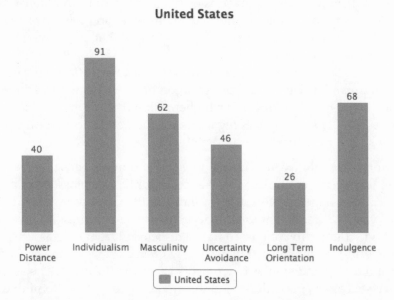

United States

And here are the full explanations that I attempted to summarize briefly in the text of the book:

Power Distance Index. Hofstede's Power Distance Index measures the extent to which the less powerful members of organizations and institutions (like the family) accept and expect that power is distributed unequally. This represents inequality (more versus less), but defined from below, not from above. It suggests that a society's level of inequality is endorsed by the followers as much as by the leaders.

---

[111] This appendix is basically an extended quote, lightly edited, from this website: www.clearlycultural.com/geert-hofstede-cultural-dimensions/individualism.

In the US, the fact that everybody is unique implies that we are all unequal. One of the most salient aspects of inequality is the degree of power each person exerts or can exert over other persons; power being defined as the degree to which a person is able to influence other people's ideas and behavior.

Individualism. Individualism is the one side versus its opposite, collectivism, that is the degree to which individuals are integrated into groups. On the individualist side we find societies in which the ties between individuals are loose: everyone is expected to look after him/herself and his/her immediate family. On the collectivist side, we find societies in which people from birth onwards are integrated into strong, cohesive in-groups, often extended families (with uncles, aunts, and grandparents) which continue protecting them in exchange for unquestioning loyalty.

The fundamental issue addressed by this dimension is the degree of interdependence a society maintains among its members. It has to do with whether people's self-image is defined in terms of "I" or "We." In Individualist societies people are supposed to look after only themselves and their direct family. In Collectivist societies people belong to "in groups" that take care of them in exchange for unquestioning loyalty.

The United States can clearly be seen as individualistic (scoring a 91). The "American dream" is clearly a representation of this. This is the Americans' hope for a better quality of life and a higher standard of living than their parents'. This belief is that anyone, regardless of their status can "pull up their boot straps" and raise themselves from poverty.

Masculinity. Masculinity versus its opposite, femininity, refers to the distribution of roles between the genders—another fundamental issue for any society to which a range of solutions is found. The IBM studies revealed that (a) women's values differ less among societies than men's values; (b) men's values from one country to another contain a dimension from very assertive and competitive and maximally different from women's values on the one side, to modest and caring and similar to women's values on the other. The assertive pole has been called "masculine" and the modest, caring pole "feminine."

A high score (Masculine) on this dimension indicates that the society will be driven by competition, achievement, and success, with success being defined by the "winner" or "best-in-the-field." This value system starts in childhood and continues throughout one's life—in both work and leisure pursuits. The fundamental issue here is what motivates people: wanting to be the best (Masculine) or liking what you do (Feminine). The score of the US on Masculinity is high at 62.

This American Masculinity plus Individualism reflects itself in the following:

- Behavior in school, work, and play is based on the shared values that people should "strive to be the best they can be" and that "the winner takes all." As a result, Americans will tend to display and talk freely about their "successes" and achievements in life. Being successful per se is not the great motivator in American society, but being able to show one's success.

- Many American assessment systems are based on precise target setting, by which American employees can show how good a job they did.

- There exists a "can-do" mentality which creates a lot of dynamism in the society, as it is believed that there is always the possibility to do things in a better way.

- Typically, Americans "live to work" so that they can obtain monetary rewards and as a consequence attain higher status based on how good one can be. Many white collar workers will move to a more fancy neighborhood after each and every substantial promotion.

- It is believed that a certain degree of conflict will bring out the best of people, as it is the goal to be "the winner." As a consequence, we see a lot of polarisation and court cases. This mentality nowadays undermines the American premise of "liberty and justice for all." Rising inequality is endangering democracy, because a widening gap among the classes may slowly push Power Distance up and Individualism down.

Uncertainty Avoidance. Uncertainty avoidance deals with a society's tolerance for uncertainty and ambiguity; it ultimately refers to the human search for Truth. It indicates to what extent a culture programs its members to feel either uncomfortable or comfortable in unstructured situations. Unstructured situations are novel, unknown, surprising, and different from usual. Uncertainty avoiding cultures try to minimize the possibility of such situations by strict laws and rules, safety and security measures, and on the philosophical and religious level by a belief in absolute Truth; "there can only be one Truth and we have it."

The dimension Uncertainty Avoidance has to do with *the way that a society deals with the fact that the future can never be known*: should we try to control the future or just let it happen? This ambiguity brings with it anxiety and different cultures have learnt to deal with this anxiety in different ways. The extent to which the members of a culture feel threatened by ambiguous or unknown situations and have created beliefs and institutions that try to avoid these is reflected in the score on Uncertainty Avoidance.

The US scores below average, with a low score of 46, on the Uncertainty Avoidance dimension. As a consequence, the perceived context in which Americans find themselves will impact their behavior more than if the culture had scored either higher or lower. In the US, there is a fair degree of acceptance for new ideas or innovative products, and a willingness to try something new or different, whether it pertains to technology, business practices, or food. Americans tend to be more tolerant of ideas or opinions from anyone and allow freedom of expression. At the same time, Americans do not require a lot of rules and are less emotionally expressive than higher-scoring cultures.

Long-Term Orientation. Long-Term Orientation is the fifth dimension of Hofstede; it was added after the original four to try to distinguish the difference in thinking between the East and West. From the original IBM studies, this difference could not be deduced. Therefore, Hofstede created a Chinese value survey which was distributed across 23 countries. From these results, and with an understanding of the influence of the teaching of Confucius on the East, long-term vs. short-term orientation became the fifth cultural dimension.

Below are some characteristics of the two opposing sides of this dimension:

Long-term orientation:

- persistence
- ordering relationships by status and observing this order
- thrift
- having a sense of shame

Short-term orientation:

- personal steadiness and stability
- protecting your "face"
- respect for tradition
- reciprocation of greetings, favors, and gifts

This dimension describes *how every society has to maintain some links with its own past while dealing with the challenges of the present and future,* and societies prioritise these two existential goals differently. Normative societies, which score low on this dimension, for example, prefer to maintain time-honored traditions and norms while viewing societal change with suspicion.

The United States scores normative with a low score of 26. American businesses measure their performance on a short-term basis, with profit and loss statements being issued on a quarterly basis. This also drives individuals to strive for quick results within the work place.

Indulgence. A tendency toward a relatively weak control over their impulses is called "Indulgence," whereas a relatively strong control over their urges is called "Restraint." Cultures can be described as Indulgent or Restrained. The United States scores as an Indulgent (68).

Appendix II: More on Gross National Happiness

I'm including this to further emphasize how holistic the underpinnings of Bhutan's system are. Essentially, the country's core is Buddhism. The Gross National Happiness (GNH) measurement is based on Buddhist principles, and from that, they have generated policy assessment tools for legislature. Because they have recently done a kind of countrywide reboot, this whole multi-layered system is very integrated and there has not yet been much in the way of cultural drift away from this core.

These are the nine Domains to GNH:

1. Psychological Wellbeing
2. Standard of Living
3. Good Governance
4. Health
5. Education
6. Community Vitality
7. Cultural Diversity and Resilience
8. Time Use
9. Ecological Diversity and Resilience

GNH serves as a kind of unifying worldview for Bhutan's five-year plans, as well as indicating how the country is doing in terms of overall health. Policy proposals are evaluated using questions devised based on these nine Domains. The particular questions asked will depend on the policy, but they include things like whether the new policy will increase or decrease stress levels for the people, and whether it will provide opportunity to learn about and participate in cultural activities. Policies that are not at least neutral (if not positive) are rejected or required to be revised before they can be further considered.

I don't know about you, but the thought of having actual criteria for policy consideration—and further that those criteria would be based on the direct impact policies would have on the welfare of the people—is shocking in its humanity.

The grossnationalhappiness.com website has a lot more information.

Appendix III: The Black Lives Matter Platform

I dedicate words to this in this book because no notion of community is whole without the liberation of all people. Black Lives Matter has done a remarkable job of articulating what that looks like in concrete terms that affect not only the liberation of black people, but all oppressed people in the US. I also invite you to notice where there is significant overlap between the BLM Platform and the one I have put together.

My sense is this is in part because people of color tend to think more in terms of "we" than "I" —which is the foundational cultural shift I see happening within intentional communities. What a "we" world looks like is obviously not identical when constructed from the perspective of a white person, but it is well worth noting how much our deep needs for reform overlap. Regardless of that overlap, however, this document is well worth studying in full, and is reprinted from the Movement for Black Lives website website (policy. m4bl.org) on January 12, 2017.

A: End the War on Black People:

We demand an end to the war against Black people. Since this country's inception there have been named and unnamed wars on our communities. We demand an end to the criminalization, incarceration, and killing of our people. This includes:

1. An immediate end to the criminalization and dehumanization of Black youth across all areas of society including, but not limited to; our nation's justice and education systems, social service agencies, and media and pop culture. This includes an end to zero-tolerance school policies and arrests of students, the removal of police from schools, and the reallocation of funds from police and punitive school discipline practices to restorative services.

2. An end to capital punishment.

3. An end to money bail, mandatory fines, fees, court surcharges, and "defendant funded" court proceedings.

4. An end to the use of past criminal history to determine eligibility for

housing, education, licenses, voting, loans, employment, and other services and needs.

5. An end to the war on Black immigrants including the repeal of the 1996 crime and immigration bills, an end to all deportations, immigrant detention, and Immigration and Custom Enforcement (ICE) raids, and mandated legal representation in immigration court.

6. An end to the war on Black trans, queer, and gender nonconforming people, including their addition to anti-discrimination civil rights protections to ensure they have full access to employment, health, housing, and education.

7. An end to the mass surveillance of Black communities, and the end to the use of technologies that criminalize and target our communities (including IMSI catchers, drones, body cameras, and predictive policing software).

8. The demilitarization of law enforcement, including law enforcement in schools and on college campuses.

9. An immediate end to the privatization of police, prisons, jails, probation, parole, food, phone, and all other criminal justice related services.

10. Until we achieve a world where cages are no longer used against our people we demand an immediate change in conditions and an end to all jails, detention centers, youth facilities, and prisons as we know them. This includes the end of solitary confinement, the end of shackling of pregnant people, access to quality healthcare, and effective measures to address the needs of our youth, queer, gender nonconforming, and trans families.

B. Reparations

We demand **reparations for past and continuing harms**. The government, responsible corporations, and other institutions that have profited off of the harm they have inflicted on Black people—from colonialism to slavery through food and housing redlining, mass incarceration, and surveillance—must repair the harm done. This includes:

1. Reparations for the systemic denial of access to high quality educational opportunities in the form of full and free access for all Black people (including undocumented and currently and formerly incarcerated people) to lifetime education including: free access and open admissions to public community colleges and universities, technical education (technology, trade, and agricultural), educational support programs, retroactive forgiveness of student loans, and support for lifetime learning programs.

2. Reparations for the continued divestment from, discrimination to-

ward, and exploitation of our communities in the form of a guaranteed minimum livable income for all Black people, with clearly articulated corporate regulations.

3. Reparations for the wealth extracted from our communities through environmental racism, slavery, food apartheid, housing discrimination, and racialized capitalism in the form of corporate and government reparations focused on healing ongoing physical and mental trauma, and ensuring our access and control of food sources, housing, and land.

4. Reparations for the cultural and educational exploitation, erasure, and extraction of our communities in the form of mandated public school curricula that critically examine the political, economic, and social impacts of colonialism and slavery, and funding to support, build, preserve, and restore cultural assets and sacred sites to ensure the recognition and honoring of our collective struggles and triumphs.

5. Legislation at the federal and state level that requires the United States to acknowledge the lasting impacts of slavery, establish and execute a plan to address those impacts. This includes the immediate passage of H.R.40, the "Commission to Study Reparation Proposals for African-Americans Act" or subsequent versions which call for reparations remedies.

C. Invest-divest

We demand **investments in the education, health, and safety of Black people**, instead of investments in the criminalizing, caging, and harming of Black people. We want investments in Black communities, determined by Black communities, and **divestment from exploitative forces** including prisons, fossil fuels, police, surveillance, and exploitative corporations. This includes:

1. A reallocation of funds at the federal, state, and local level from policing and incarceration (JAG, COPS, VOCA) to long-term safety strategies such as education, local restorative justice services, and employment programs.

2. The retroactive decriminalization, immediate release, and record expungement of all drug related offenses and prostitution, and reparations for the devastating impact of the "war on drugs" and criminalization of prostitution, including a reinvestment of the resulting savings and revenue into restorative services, mental health services, job programs, and other programs supporting those impacted by the sex and drug trade.

3. Real, meaningful, and equitable universal health care that guarantees:

proximity to nearby comprehensive health centers, culturally competent services for all people, specific services for queer, gender nonconforming, and trans people, full bodily autonomy, full reproductive services, mental health services, paid parental leave, and comprehensive quality child and elder care.

4. A constitutional right at the state and federal level to a fully-funded education which includes a clear articulation of the right to: a free education for all, special protections for queer and trans students, wrap-around services, social workers, free health services (including reproductive body autonomy), a curriculum that acknowledges and addresses students' material and cultural needs, physical activity and recreation, high quality food, free daycare, and freedom from unwarranted search, seizure, or arrest.

5. A divestment from industrial multinational use of fossil fuels and investment in community-based sustainable energy solutions.

6. A cut in military expenditures and a reallocation of those funds to invest in domestic infrastructure and community well-being.

D. Economic Justice

We demand **economic justice for all** and a reconstruction of the economy to ensure Black communities have collective ownership, not merely access. This includes:

1. A progressive restructuring of tax codes at the local, state, and federal levels to ensure a radical and sustainable redistribution of wealth.

2. Federal and state job programs that specifically target the most economically marginalized Black people, and compensation for those involved in the care economy. Job programs must provide a living wage and encourage support for local workers' centers, unions, and Black-owned businesses which are accountable to the community.

3. A right to restored land, clean air, clean water, and housing and an end to the exploitative privatization of natural resources—including land and water. We seek democratic control over how resources are preserved, used, and distributed and do so while honoring and respecting the rights of our indigenous family.

4. The right for workers to organize in public and private sectors especially in "On Demand Economy" jobs.

5. Restore the Glass-Steagall Act to break up the large banks, and call for the National Credit Union Administration and the US Department of the Treasury to change policies and practices around regulation, reporting, and consolidation to allow for the continuation and creation

of black banks, small and community development credit unions, insurance companies, and other financial institutions.

6. An end to the Trans-Pacific Partnership and a renegotiation of all trade agreements to prioritize the interests of workers and communities.

7. Through tax incentives, loans, and other government directed resources, support the development of cooperative or social economy networks to help facilitate trade across and in Black communities globally. All aid in the form of grants, loans, or contracts to help facilitate this must go to Black led or Black supported networks and organizations as defined by the communities.

8. Financial support of Black alternative institutions including policy that subsidizes and offers low-interest, interest-free, or federally guaranteed low-interest loans to promote the development of cooperatives (food, residential, etc.), land trusts, and culturally responsive health infrastructures that serve the collective needs of our communities.

9. Protections for workers in industries that are not appropriately regulated including domestic workers, farm workers, and tipped workers, and for workers—many of whom are Black women and incarcerated people—who have been exploited and remain unprotected. This includes the immediate passage at the federal and state level of the Domestic Workers' Bill of Rights and extension of worker protections to incarcerated people.

E. Community Control

We demand a world where those most impacted in our **communities control the laws, institutions, and policies that are meant to serve us**—from our schools to our local budgets, economies, police departments, and our land—while recognizing that the rights and histories of our indigenous family must also be respected. This includes:

1. Direct democratic community control of local, state, and federal law enforcement agencies, ensuring that communities most harmed by destructive policing have the power to hire and fire officers, determine disciplinary action, control budgets and policies, and subpoena relevant agency information.

2. An end to the privatization of education and real community control by parents, students, and community members of schools including democratic school boards and community control of curriculum, hiring, firing, and discipline policies.

3. Participatory budgeting at the local, state, and federal level.

F. Political Power

We demand **independent Black political power and Black self-determination** in all areas of society. We envision a remaking of the current US political system in order to create a real democracy where Black people and all marginalized people can effectively exercise full political power. This includes:

1. An end to the criminalization of Black political activity including the immediate release of all political prisoners and an end to the repression of political parties.

2. Public financing of elections and the end of money controlling politics through ending super PACs and unchecked corporate donations.

3. Election protection, electoral expansion, and the right to vote for all people including: full access, guarantees, and protections of the right to vote for all people through universal voter registration, automatic voter registration, pre-registration for 16-year-olds, same-day voter registration, voting day holidays, Online Voter Registration (OVR), enfranchisement of formerly and presently incarcerated people, local and state resident voting for undocumented people, and a ban on any disenfranchisement laws.

4. Full access to technology including net neutrality and universal access to the internet without discrimination and full representation for all.

5. Protection and increased funding for Black institutions including Historically Black Colleges and Universities (HBCU's), Black media, and cultural, political, and social formations.